THE LIT___ ____ ____

OF NUMEROLOGY:

The Science of Names, Numbers and the Law of Vibration

BY VIOLET ROY

FOREWORD

Do you desire to be healthy, wealthy or popular —a real success?
Do you want to get a new lease on life, become the life of the
party, and bring both pleasure and profit?

Then this book is written for you.

Would you be the center of attraction in any group? Tell each one
something about himself. You will have his immediate attention.
Attention creates interest, and once you have his interest, the world
is yours, and everything in it.

As a popular means of entertainment and a scientific method for
achieving success, you will find Numerology a subject worthwhile.
It is an old, old science, yet like many other new things which
become the theme of the hour, seeks merely to remove the dust
from one of our most valuable antiques, more ancient than the
pyramids or the tomb of King Tut—the Law of Vibration as
applied to Name and Birth Date—and bring it forth to the light,
where its true value may be appreciated, under-stood, and linked
with modern usage.

You as an individual have a certain rate of vibration determined by
the numerical value of the letters in your name. This in turn is
based on the fundamental truth taught by Pythagoras, now held by
modern scientists, that everything is of one substance, and that this
one substance, in different rates of vibration, produces all the
various manifestations of life. "Sound creates form, resistance
color, while thoughts are merely things vibrating at a higher rate of
speed."

Language and mathematics being our chief means of
communicating thought, the digits and letters of the alphabet bear a
close relation to each other. Pythagoras held that each digit had a
certain influence, tone and color, affecting in like manner all things
to which it was related, and that each letter of the alphabet, by

2

reason of its numerical position, had the particular characteristics of its controlling vibration.

The Value of Numerology to You.

Numerology gives you a knowledge of the law which governs your life. It enables you to attract success now instead of waiting for that big opportunity in the elusive future.

As a lover or spouse, it may help you understand your other half and their respective love language or way of engaging with you.

As a parent, you will find it an invaluable aid in handling your children – especially if he or she has a mind of their own. It gives you a peep behind the scenes, into the child's own mind, and thus you have at once the key to the situation.

As a teacher, it will give you an understanding of each individual pupil and increase your success in a surprising manner, affording a most efficient method for the scientific study of human nature in all its varied aspects.

As a businessperson, it enables you to find your true vocation and thus save money and time in "arriving" at the top of the success ladder. As a salesman, it provides you with a forehand knowledge of your customer and shows the proper stimuli to apply in order to obtain the desired reaction.

As a business man, it gives you a tip as to the best-selling mediums and the most advantageous days for developing and promoting the various angles of your line.

As a manufacturer, putting a new article on the market, it enables you to attract success from the universal ether by use of the right vibratory name, thus assuring its appeal to the certain class of people whom you wish to reach.

As a numerologist, this work affords you the most wonderful aid of any work in print. With over 1,500 indexed names, giving their vowel, consonant and total values, you have the largest store of information that has ever been compiled for this purpose. It will save you hours of time, and in addition thereto will enable you to give your client a choice in the selection of an efficient name. This in turn is bound to react to your benefit from every success standpoint.

As an artist, you have a list of over 1,500 names from which to select a winning nom de plume.

As a writer, the indexed list of names gives you scientific material from which to choose your characters, thus making them absolutely true to life.

As a student of the occult, this text gives you the answer to the eternal questions, "Whence, why and whither?" as well as to many things which have been a subject of won-der: "Why is A I ?" How does my name affect me?" "How do I attract my own happiness and success?" "How may I gain the help and protection of the universal forces?" Whoever you are, whatever your problem, Numerology will help you to a better understanding of life. When you discover why things are as they are and why certain people react as they do, your perplexities will begin to dissolve and the sun will shine once more in your locality.

The most exact of all sciences is mathematics. The medium of thought is language. Based on the truth of reincarnation, Numerology correlates the universal value of numbers with the rules of language and the law of vibration and gives to each individual a picture of his former self, his present status in life, and points the way to his highest goal.

If you desire to get the most out of life now, adjust yourself, through your name, to your own birth-path forces. Then all the universe vibrates with you and for you, work will be a pleasure and joy will attend each day.

Numerology is the most enjoyable route by which to gain a knowledge of the greatest law of the universe,—vibration,—which, when put into operation in your individual affairs, will bring order out of chaos and cause harmony, peace and happiness to reign supreme in your environment. It opens at once the door to greater opportunity. Seize it now.

The why of this science is a study in philosophy and metaphysics, but the universal meaning of the numbers never fails to be of absorbing interest to those who have learned their A, B, Cs. We trust that the pleasure and benefit derived from applying the rules in this new game of life will make you want to know more of the fascinating subject, portraying YOU—Past, Present and Future.

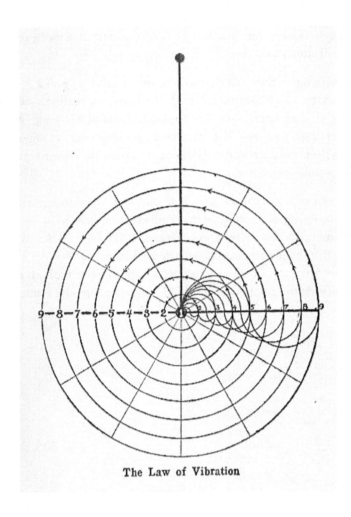

The Law of Vibration

Numerology Made Plain

NOTE : If you are in a hurry, you will find the quickest method of analysis in Chapter XV.

CHAPTER I

YOUR NAME: A METAPHYSICAL PORTRAIT OF YOU

DID you ever stop to think that your name, whether spoken (sound vibration) or written (a certain arrangement of letters, transferred to the brain by color vibration), immediately registers upon the mind of the receiver a mental picture of yourself, with all of your most prominent characteristics standing out in bold relief?

Your name broadcasts you to the universe. It gives an entire stranger thousands of miles away an insight into your subconscious mind, a knowledge of your talents, disposition and range of intellect.

Your name pictures you—all you have been and are at the present moment. It is your trademark, advertising to the world your own particular brand of success. Does it stand for efficiency as does the Energizer Bunny?

You are to the world what your name portrays. It leaves an indelible impression on your environment and associates, causing some to immediately like you (if they have harmonious vibrations) and others to avoid you. If you wish to know in what esteem you are held by acquaintances and friends, just figure out the various nicknames by which you have been labeled.

If William be your business signature, the one who receives your letter knows at once (if he knows the law of numbers) that you are a man with decided opinions of your own. You stand for principle, you finish what you undertake, you can be relied upon to keep your word, yet you have such an independent spirit that you do not take kindly to any suggestions from others. He will have to proceed tactfully and make you feel that you really know best how this deal should be handled. In asking your advice instead of advising you, he will strike a responsive chord which will arouse in you an interest in his proposition.

If Bill is your trademark, one can be more frank and open —your feelings are not so easily hurt. You are one of those "hail fellows well met," with physical magnetism and mental diplomacy, which make you an unusually splendid "driver." You can be depended upon to put the deal over though you have to fight for your rights every step of the way. You'll be just in your dealings, willing to meet the other fellow half way, yet he knows before he starts that his arguments must be sane and sound, practical and to the point, if he does not wish to return home with his armor punched full of holes. In the commercial world you're the "Big Boss," able to "make it pay," and if you are really doing big things, and not too grasping for personal fame, the chances are you'll have more money than William or Will.

If your original name has shortened to Will, you are refined, cultured, artistic, hiding the stubborn streak of William under an outer garb of diplomacy. You have not the fighting qualities of Bill nor his keen sense of values, but you have infinitely more patience, a greater deference for public opinion, and much more style.

But if the fellows call you "Bill" and your wife says "Will," take it for granted that she considers you of much finer clay than do the boys with whom you travel. She may love you dearly, yet she will not "mind," and will be inclined to have things go her way. If you wish to be the "boss" yourself, train her to say "Bill, dear" (before she reads this paragraph).

Why the differences? Vibration.

Changing the spelling of your name makes you a different person because it changes your rate of vibration.

CHAPTER II

WHAT IS VIBRATION?

YOUR breath is one vibration—inhaling and exhaling —a positive movement with a reflex action. The Century Dictionary says that vibration is "a movement to and fro," or "oscillation," as the forward and backward swing of the pendulum of a clock.

Modern science says that "all life is vibration," and that without vibration there would be no life.

The first breath of life, when spirit entered matter, set into motion or vibration universal forces of creative, energy.

You cannot limit the flow of energy in any form without causing an entirely new aspect to arise. Stop the flow of blood in any portion of the body,—congestion immediately follows and causes a lump to appear. Build a dam across a stream and you soon have a goodsized reservoir.

Turn on the faucet and let the water run. The bowl will soon be full, from whence the stream will continue its course until it meets with an opposite force or certain boundaries. When the space thus found has been filled to the original water level a new outlet is sought, then another and another.

The accompanying illustration will serve to show how in like manner the great creative force, through the medium of vibration, continues to. activate larger and larger spheres of activity.

Let the large circle represent the naught or chaos from which the universe emerged. The first manifestation of life was the dot within the circle. While the earth is not the center of the universe, it is the concentrated center of our activities, and so we shall consider the dot in the, center of the accompanying sketch as the earth in its primal form.

'We shall not relate the various steps in evolution which led up to Adam or the first man. These are found in the first chapter of Genesis. We are concerned primarily with Man from the time that he became imbued with spirit and thus became a reflection of the Universal Intelligence.

The entry of spirit into matter caused a new influx of creative energy to send its vibrations in all directions. Just as a pebble thrown into the water starts a succession of circular ripples around it, each individual wave going an equal distance above and below the water level, so did the first vibration or movement of spirit in matter cause everything to manifest a dual aspect.

The Origin of the Digits

In the human kingdom, the positive movement of this first vibration is typified by Adam, the first man. As soon as he arrived at perfection the negative or feminine counterpart appeared in Eve, the first woman. With the completion of this second unit of energy the great creative force continued to pour its rhythmic current through the dual aspect of the first vibration until a third expression of life appeared. Now we have father-mother-child, or man, woman and the magnetic attraction between them—complete expression.

Thus did life progress, each positive current of energy being followed by its corresponding reverse aspect, these two producing an ever-higher expression, while the particular manifestations which characterized each successive step became the symbols of the primary units of energy which produced them. In the course of time these symbols, the nine digits, became the foundation of all calculation and exchange and grew into the most exact of all sciences, Mathematics.

While languages and alphabets vary, numbers have maintained a uniformity of shape and a definite value throughout the world, showing that they are based on certain universal principles. The particular meaning attached to each digit may be found by a study of the ancient Jewish Kabbala, the sacred writings of the Chinese or the science of Numerology as taught by Pythagoras, each one symbolizing certain stages of growth as the universe and man evolved.

All life being a continuous flow of energy from the One Original Source, each primary unit of vibration continues to transmit its special attributes through the medium of its respective agent, the digit, to anything in the universe which has its number value, giving to such individual, principle or thing the characteristics peculiar to its specific rate of vibration.

CHAPTER III

VIBRATION APPLIED TO THE ALPHABET

ATTACHING numbers to the 26 letters of the alphabet in the order of sequence, we find that eventually each one comes under the influence of one of the nine digits:

A	B	C	D	E	F	G	H	I
1	2	3	4	5	6	7	8	9
J	K	L	M	N	O	P	Q	R
10	11	12	13	14	15	16	17	18
1	2	3	4	5	6	7	8	9
S	T	U	V	W	X	Y	Z	
19	20	21	22	23	24	25	26	
1Ø	2	3	4	5	6	7	8	

Why is A1?

Right here you have a right to ask, as have the most intelligent men the writer has known: "Admitting the truth of what you say as to our particular characteristics, how do you arrive at such conclusions? Why is A 1? "

The letters of our alphabet have stood in their particular order of succession for hundreds of years and have long since absorbed the universal characteristics which are transmitted by the respective digits to all things having their particular number value or rate of vibration.

Other Alphabets

"Granting even that, how does this vibratory law ap-ply to other languages, when the alphabet is not the same and the letters stand in a different order?"

The law of vibration is universal in its application.

Anything which a number or digit determines will take on the aspects of that vibration when it has been under such influence for a long enough period of time to have absorbed such qualities into its nature.

The law applies to each alphabet as it stands, the difference in word values showing a fine distinction in the way different nationalities have grown to regard the same thing. Take for example the letters of the Hebrew alphabet, which in the order of sequence stood for certain steps in the evolution of the Cosmos as do the nine digits. Do you think for one moment that the ancient Hebrew, if transplanted here, would view any one thing in our modern existence in the same light as the average man of today?

Hence, taking into consideration the time element, a new vibration or change of name will not affect an individual immediately unless his or her inner self has grown to meet it. They must wear it long enough to absorb the universal vibrations behind it before it really becomes a part of their nature.

How the Digits Influence Our Alphabet

The twenty-six letters of our alphabet, having stood in their present numerical order for centuries, have absorbed the qualities of their controlling digits,

1. 1 transmitting its particular aspect of universal intelligence to the letters A, J, S, giving them creative powers, with initiative, daring, independence and the pioneer spirit.
2. 2 giving to B, K, T diplomacy and tact, with imitative and collective qualities.
3. 3 causing C, L, U to find joyous expression in art or humanitarian lines.

4. 4 endowing D, M, V with a good intellect, a conscientious sense of duty and enjoyment of life in work or study.

5. 5 bringing many changes to E, N, W, making them ((gogetters" for experience—versatile, active and charming.

6. 6 making F, 0, X the best mothers, teachers and human benefactors.

7. 7 throwing spiritual qualities over G, P, Y, with a desire for perfection, wisdom and authority.

8. 8 bringing money to H, Q, Z when they direct their energies wisely and unselfishly, with justice and tact.

9. 9 giving I and R success in art, literature and the healing profession, with the entire world for their field of expression.

In addition to the nine digits we have two master numbers,-11 and 22,—which throw leadership qualities around the other numbers to which they are related.

11 stands for a new beginning in a higher cycle, a greater spiritual unfoldment, with inspirational and psychic qualities.

22 is considered the highest vibration of all, being represented in the universe by the Trinity, 3, the 7 planets and the 12 signs of the zodiac. 3 plus 7 plus 12 is 22. 22 links the spiritual with the material and makes inspirational things practical, directing large enterprises with diplomacy and tact.

Numbers Applied to the Name

Take the name David Wark Griffith, a famous movie producer, and attach the number value of each letter (using the table shown on the first page of this chapter).

Place the digits representing the vowels above, the consonants below, and the full name on a separate line, adding the digits of each name separately and then altogether.

```
                 1    +   1   +      9   = (11)—Soul—talents.
                10                  18
Vowels:         1  9      1      9   9
             DAVID     WARK    GRIFFITH
Consonants: 4  4   4   5  9 2   7 9 6 6 2 8
                12        16        38
                 3         7        11
                       10                    = (1-11)—Body—
                                                    personality.
Full name:  4 1 4 9 4  5 1 9 2  7 9 9 6 6 9 2 8
                          1 7       56
             2 2           8        11    = (22-8-11)—Intellect
                                                 and destiny.
```

All double numbers are reduced to single numbers by the addition of their digits with the exception of 11 and 22, the master vibrations. These always stand out by themselves, expressing their leadership qualities through the smaller numbers to which they are related.

The above name is an unusual example of the far-reaching influence of an individual who has master numbers in every position—vowels, consonants and full name.

The 'vowels of your full name reveal your natural talents—those things in which you have previously scored success, and which are now stored within the realm of your subconscious mind.

The vowel digits of 1-1-9 above, which total 11, indicate that Mr. Griffith in a previous lifetime was undoubtedly a promoter and leader (11), a pioneer (1) and inventive genius (1) in the field of art or humanitarian (9) endeavor. This would give him a natural ambition to excel in such lines now and to think in world (9) terms.

Your consonants represent the physical body through which your mind in expressing. They reveal your personality—the impression you make upon others.

The above consonant vibration of (1-11) shows that Mr. Griffith is a dynamic, enthusiastic individual who cares naught for precedent or what other folks may think. The 3 of David shows his appreciation of the beautiful and artistic; the 7 of Wark, his eye for detail, perfection and finish, while the 11 of Griffith immediately stamps him as a leader in any field, interested in something "different," something large, yet having an inspirational or uplifting effect.

Your full name shows the intellectual growth you have made in previous lifetimes and indicates the destiny which you have now come to fulfill.

The above name has two master numbers in the individual name totals; so we do not add the 3 names together and obtain a final total, as is usually the case.

The total digits of (22-8-11) indicate that Mr. Griffith came to earth this time endowed with a most powerful intellect with which to work out a destiny of universal magnitude. The 22 shows ability to analyze and organize the inspirational ideas of the 11 vibration and carry them out in an executive, forceful, money-making, successful (8) manner.

The leadership qualities of 11 and 22 make this individual an unusual business (8) engineer (8) in the line of dramatic art, where the imitative qualities of 8 combine with the innate artistic expression of 9. Mr. Griffith must work with a big, immense idea to be a genuine success, for his are universal vibrations. A limited environment or sphere of action would cause his own strong forces to revert disastrously upon him. "To whom much is given, from him shall much be required." Mr. Griffith's unparalleled success shows that fortune and fame await those who have the courage to live up to the demands of their own high vibrations.

CHAPTER IV

THE STORY OF THE NUMBERS

EACH letter of your name, by reason of its numerical position in the alphabet, has a certain rate of vibration. Each vibration has certain characteristics. Therefore, you as an individual are a composite of all the qualities which the letters of your name symbolize, the highest number in your name indicating your present stage of growth or development.

This is not your first appearance on the earth planet. You have been here before, each time with a new lesson to learn. The various stages through which you have passed are revealed by the O. The cipher or naught stands for the period of chaos before time began. It also symbolizes the boundless space from which all things came forth. The first manifestation of life was the dot within the circle, "representing the sun in the center of the zodiac, the giver of light, life and energy to its system. . . . Every unit of life is the center or dot or its own universe, has its own sphere of activity and influence, and the rate of vibration." (Key to the Universe, Curtiss, pp. 57, 59.)

1. The first manifestation of motion in the Cosmos, or spirit coming down into matter, is symbolized by the straight line. It represents the primal cause and stands for the principle of unity in all things. "1 cannot be divided; multiplied by itself it still maintains its unity, yet it creates all others." Thus we have creative ability, daring and the pioneer spirit symbolized by the digit 1.

2. The first vibration, generated by the contact of spirit with matter, is typified in its positive aspect by Adam, the first

man, followed by Eve, his feminine or negative counterpart, gaining her way by artful diplomacy. Thus we have two units of energy representing the complete expression of the first vibration, giving to the digit 2 the qualities of duality, diplomacy and a receptive, feminine nature.

3. The great creative force working through the two aspects of the first vibration produced a third unit of ex-pression. Thus 3 marks the completion of the first earth-trinity, father-mother-child, and stands for complete and joyous expression on the nature plane.

4. Having attained physical perfection, man found that after all he was not quite satisfied. He looked about and began to wonder why. He started to reason things out for himself and thus evolved his intellect. He found that lasting good only came to him when he him-self was. "on the square." Proof of one principle gave him a burning desire for more until we find him early and late striving to make more money with which to further pursue the path of intellectual attainment. A true 4 is always busy, energetic and on the square, ever seeking more proof and greater knowledge.

5. Arrived at a stage of mental supremacy, the individual longed to try his powers. In doing so he met with many varied experiences and some bitter lessons until he made the big discovery which restored to him his balance. He found that knowledge alone was not sufficient to bring his heart's desire and that only when absolute master of self and all his physical passions could he dominate others through his own magnetic powers. To know life from every angle with unbounded freedom of thought and action is the constant desire of 5.

6. Having, like the prodigal son, traveled in a far country and drunk his fill, the 5 individual decides to return home and settle down. He concludes that life after all is what we make it and every responsibility has its corresponding reward. Domestic life "looks good" to him; so he establishes a home and raises a family, which develops his backbone. He becomes a prime factor in the promotion of education, health and human betterment in his community, deriving a keen enjoyment from the free advice he gives to others. The sterling qualities gained here are found in mothers, teachers, doctors, welfare workers and all others who stand as guardians of the home, school and society, in whose names the 6 vibration is usually strong.

7. Having worked hard to rear his family, educate them and fit them to take their place in society, the 7 individual feels that he is entitled to a rest from manual labor. He seeks out a quiet place in nature and sits down to think things over. After all, is there not something more to be attained? He knows the road that he has come; he has left no details undone to reach his present state of perfection. He is sure of himself in this respect and resents any suggestions from others. Yet his intuition tells him that there surely must be some higher laws than those of the purely material world, which laws, if put into operation in daily affairs, would bring results much quicker. He acts on his hunch and begins to study the occult and metaphysical laws on which he formerly looked with disfavor. He sees at once that the higher law must always include the lesser and begins to figure out how things can be done without so much mental and physical effort. Wonderful ideas present themselves to his inner searching mind. Here is the wisdom for which he has been searching, which he now must tell to all mankind. Hence, we find many preachers,

teachers and religious and metaphysical writers predominating in the 7 vibration.

8. Having gathered a store of mystical lore with which to enhance his fortunes, the 7 individual is asked by many who hear him so eloquently expound, "Have you proved these principles out for yourself? Do you know by experience 'just what they are worth?" 8, being an honest soul, with good fighting qualities and a keen sense of justice, determines to show his materially-minded friends the concrete proof of what he preaches, so he enters again the commercial world and puts his theories into practice. They stand the test, and he finds that rest after all was not what he wanted. He goes to work with added zeal to make his declarations real and finds that a perfect balance of wisdom and work, love and justice, ideas and materials, plus an intelligent driving force, brings money, success and fame by a much shorter route than his purely laborious reasoning efforts. Thus 8 becomes the "big business" man, the large executive, tempering reason with intuition, justice with love and force with diplomacy.

9. Increased material success having come through the use of the higher laws in the material world, the individual realizes that even with money and fame he is not entirely happy. He notes the trouble and lack, so totally unnecessary, in the lives of those about him, and develops a sympathetic interest in their welfare. His positive efforts to help the other fellow to a higher understanding of life attract a reflex current of thankfulness and good will, bringing in their wake more wealth and a greater enjoyment of life than when he worked in the 8 vibration. The inspiration which comes to the 9 who truly loves his fellowman enables him to express his splendid artistic talents in a more universal way. Opportunity for extended travel comes to him, with attendant growth and renown. Famous

singers, artists and world travelers are generally strong in the number 9.

10. Having passed through the varied experiences of the 9 vibrations, man stops to survey the road he has traveled. He is a wiser man than when he started. With a knowledge of all his past joys and sorrows stored within his subconscious mind he now stands ready and strong to proceed on his way, but before he can enter a larger field he has certain tests to pass. He must prove he has learned his lessons well, and that through his knowledge of the higher laws he can create out of his own aura, if need be, all things needful for his supply. Here his friends may think him queer, he may meet with loss and adversity, in order to test his mettle, yet he must firmly stand his ground. As 10 has a wealth of inner wisdom, he must take the advice of none save the still small voice within if he desires to enter a higher cycle and enjoy success that is real and lasting.

11. Having stood the tests of aloneness, adversity and financial stress which often beset the 10 vibration, and having come out on top, man is allowed to make a new beginning in a larger field of activity. Here his subconscious mind, stored with the knowledge of all the past, enables him to speak and act inspirationally. He immediately knows how a thing should be done, though he may not be able to tell you why. This is the reason that a boy or girl with an 11 vibration in the name generally has trouble with the teacher. He thinks he knows best. His soul has grown to the point of mastery and he will not accept commands from others. He can only be reached by persuasion and an appeal to his own superior self. It is important, indeed, that he be well grounded in education and the higher laws of life, else disaster will follow in his path by reason of his strong force going in the wrong direction. An 11 is a

dynamic individual, with enthusiasm, inspiration and ideds7 which he must give out to others if he desires a reflex of good himself.

12. Having made a new beginning in a higher cycle, the individual passes through the next or twelfth grade in school. Here he has the triangle of complete expression represented 4 times (4 X3). He has gained mastery on all planes, the digits of the number itself forming the complete triangle of 1-2-3 (12 is 1 plus 2, which equals 3). In 3 man attained physical perfection; in 8, physical and mental; in 9, physical, mental and emotional; in 11, physical, mental, emotional and spiritual, while 12 includes them „all, being the number of numerical completion shown by the 12 months of the year, the 12 signs of the zodiac, etc.

13-20. From this point man goes by successive stages through the lessons of the 13, 14, 15, 16, 17 and 18, similar in nature to those of the first nine vibrations, yet with greater creative force and a farther-reaching influence. At 19 he has another testing period before being allowed to start on the first round of the third and higher cycle, signified by 20.

21.   In 1 and 2 we had the masculine and feminine in their individual aspects; in 12 we found man and woman working together, with man directing the activities of the opposite sex, but in 21, the beginning of the third cycle of evolution, we find conditions reversed, and the woman in the lead. The individual has now gained perfection in three worlds (21 is 3 X 7), physical, mental and spiritual, and is called upon to exercise his powers. When a man reaches the age of 21 he is considered an individual of discretion, capable of using the ballot wisely.

22.   Twenty-two represents the illumined intellect, where man, through the use of his perfected powers, becomes absolute master of his own environment. 22 equals

2   plus 2, or 4. 4 has the knowledge of 1, 2 and 3 plus his own additional wisdom. Hence 4 equals 1 plus 2 plus

3   plus 4, which is 10, or the foundation of a never-ending spiral of manifestation. Having grown wise through suffering, man has learned to know and obey the higher laws, by which he makes his dreams come true and his inspirational ideas develop into practical realities. He has learned how to co-operate intelligently. While in 21 the feminine aspect was in the lead, in 22 we have the perfect balance of man and woman and their joint creations, each allowing to the other perfect freedom of thought and action.

MASTER

4 1 12 5 9

Until man is master of himself and his environment he cannot be truly a wise counselor to others. Those who have come to earth with a master number (11 or 22) in their name have been through all of the first nine grades. They are here now to shed their light on souls less developed than themselves. A real 22 is often found in diplomatic circles or as a humanitarian adviser of the highest order, where his inspiration and psychic qualities, combined with his understanding, tact and executive ability, make him a leader to be reckoned with in any situation.

22 gains success through knowing the law, putting it into operation and then passing such knowledge on. When he has gained mastery over all things here he undoubtedly will find new worlds to conquer.

Warning to the High Numbers

If you have an 8, 9, 11 or 22 in the digits of your name or birth date you have passed through the 7 vibration, where you reached the peak of accomplishment for self alone. You must now work for the good of many and enlarge your interests to take in the whole world. You have developed a strong and powerful force, which must be used in an equally large manner. No matter how conscientious you may be, if you confine your activities to your own family circle or small group of associates, you are inviting disaster upon yourself. It is like trying to put 22 pounds of steam pressure into a boiler built for only 7. An explosion is bound to occur. The high numbers are meant to help the lower and bring them up to their own high plane of understanding. When they do not act in this capacity, they dig their own graves and conduct their own funerals.

Life is growth, and growth is ever upward and outward: We must keep on going. There is no such thing as standing still. The law of vibration is the law of opposites. If we do not go forward we are pushed out of the way to make room for someone else. "If we refuse to ,take a firm stand on the positive side of good, we are swept into the opposite current." (Curtiss.)

CHAPTER V

THREEFOLD MEANING OF THE DIGITS

WE have found that the law of vibration is the law of opposites. We can swing as far in one direction as in the other. The stronger our force, the greater our power for good or ill. Midway between the two extremes there is a point of negativity where the individual may be called "lukewarm"—he is neither hot nor cold. Such a person becomes the prey of the more positive minds about him and attracts trouble and loss through his own inertia.

The universal meaning of the numbers in their positive, reverse and negative aspects is given below. In the Cycle of Nature we have the triangle of 1-2-3; in the Cycle of Man, the square of 4-5-6-7, and in the Cycle of Superman, the reflection of the 1-2-3 principle 4 times in the triangles of 10-8-9, 11-8-9, 10-22-9, 11-22-9.

THE CYCLE OF NATURE: 1-2-3 The Digit 1

POSITIVE—Creative ability, originality, individuality, in-tuition, concentration, aspiration, independence, aggressiveness, initiative, strong intellect, and a daring pioneer spirit, with unity of thought and action characterizing all activities. Inventors, pioneers, promoters are found in the 1 vibration.

1 is a part of every number and hence exerts a strong influence over all other vibrations. Should a name be made up of the digits 31, as in Mary (3) Pickford (1), it would show creative ability in the field of art and self-expression (3); if it were made up of the digits 4-1, it would indicate originality in mechanical design or a builder of efficiency systems.

REVERSE—A reverse 1 is arrogant, domineering, egotistical, inconsiderate, selfish, self-centered, determined upon own satisfaction, irrespective of others.

NEGATIVE—A negative 1 is dependent, weak, lazy, sub-missive, mentally asleep, limited in thought, action and expression.

The Digit 2

POSITIVE—Duality. Even in its positive aspect 2 stands for duality. It can exercise the strong qualities of 1 and be alert and aggressive or operate through the more sociable, diplomatic and feminine side of its nature. It is co-operative, kind, a collector and builder—an excellent compiler of statistics, data and information for others to handle.

REVERSE—Critical, nagging, fault-finding, always worrying about what other people may think, posing for effect, susceptible to flattery, selfish, unreliable, too proud for own good.

NEGATIVE—Indifferent, careless, no pride in personal appearance, unsociable, unable to make up his mind on anything and stick to it, so negative and impressionable that he becomes the tool of stronger minds about him.

The Digit 3

POSITIVE—Complete and joyous expression in art or humanitarian lines—a child of nature. 3 is master on the material plane, combining the creative ability of 1 with the building and collective powers of 2 into a happy expression of those things which make for comfort, health and pleasure. He knows how to promote his own personal ambitions through the initiative of 1 and the tact of 2, excelling in music, art, literature, law, nursing and the healing profession, or in any avenue which calls for self-expression in service to others. We find many 3s associated with tea rooms, beauty parlors, millinery and gift shops. Their sense of humor and agility in repartee make them popular as toastmasters and afterdinner speakers. REVERSE—Selfish, sensual, debased, scattering forces, living alone, impatient, important, egotistical.

NEGATIVE—Repressed, unsociable, unreliable, careless in dress, unresponsive to music or art, dependent, lazy and indifferent.

THE CYCLE OF MAN: 4-5-6-7

The Digit 4

POSITIVE—Builders on material and intellectual planes) conscientious, "on the square," always busy, mentally and physically. 4 makes a splendid bookkeeper or mechanic; he is mathematical, methodical, analytical, reasoning, honest, a master of detail and routine. He is a splendid builder of systems for greater economy, efficiency or output. His ambitions are of a personal nature, for his own self-development, yet of all employees he is the most conscientious and faithful.

REVERSE—Critical, self-limited, a drudge and hard worker, with his nose to the grindstone, so economical that he makes the eagle scream, so analytical that he refuses to listen to his hunch but reasons himself out of his good intentions.

NEGATIVE—Despondent, buried beneath adverse circumstances, financial limitations and hard work, a plodder without any desire for intellectual development.

The Digit 5

POSITIVE—"Go-getters" for experience—investigators of life from every angle. 5 is a lover of freedom, change, variety, new scenes and new contacts, versatile, magnetic, charming, a good mixer, a splendid judge of human nature, interested in philosophical and metaphysical research, a good character analyst. 5 is strongly sexed, yet master of himself and able to quickly adjust himself to any environment. He is a rejuvenator and enthusiasmgenerator on all planes —the traveling salesman, the vaudeville player, the "noted lecturer on psychology."
REVERSE—Dominated by sex, here today and gone to-morrow,

always looking for greener pastures, absolutely unreliable, the destroyer of homes, peace and pleasure for selfish gratification, interested in black magic.

NEGATIVE—Physical, mental and financial failures, living a life of monotony and hardship, the result of their own self-indulgence and instability.

The Digit 6

POSITIVE—Guardians of the home, school and society, assuming responsibility graciously. A 6 is a natural mother, a splendid teacher, or a good business man, always interested in the welfare of others, although he clings closely to his own family circle. He is energetic, absolutely reliable, a good money-maker, a splendid talker-if he does not talk too much.) Many literary and professional people, especially in healing lines, are found in this vibration.

REVERSE—One of those who will argue "until the cows come home" without being able to get the other fellow's point of view; anxious, worried, self-centered, so wrapped up in "his own" that he does not care to bother with others. His obstinacy causes others to leave him alone, and, being one of those individuals who simply must talk with someone, he becomes blue and depressed. He feels that others do not appreciate his efforts to share their responsibilities. When he learns to stay in his own yard he will be a much happier individual.

NEGATIVE—Overburdened with too many cares; the "goat" for the rest of the family, the office force, or un-appreciative friends; lacking in self-esteem, indifferent as to his personal appearance.

The Digit 7

POSITIVE "Reservoirs of wisdom" who have to be ((pumped" before you really discover their depth. 7 stands for perfection, finish, culture, poise, self-confidence, attention to detail, and a firm, positive will. 7 is sensitive and proud, inclined to hold himself somewhat aloof from the common crowd, hiding his hurt feelings beneath an outer cloak of cold indifference. He can be generous, gracious and affable; at other times he desires to be left strictly alone, to meditate undisturbed. He is a lover of nature, intuitive, psychic, interested in the mystical and occult. He keeps his own counsel and the confidence of others, yet because of his secretive disposition is often lonesome and misunderstood. He must learn to say what he thinks and "get it off his chest" if he wishes to live in a happy environment. A 7 should work in an individual capacity where he is absolute authority in his own realm. He can do well in the professions, in real estate, agriculture or the religious and metaphysical world.

REVERSE—Domineering, dictatorial, restless, roving, leaving things undone, failing to keep appointments, stubborn, opinionated, atheistic, satirical, with no appreciation of the finer things of life and no leniency nor sympathy for the other fellow's views.

NEGATIVE—Lacking in self-confidence, unable to express what he feels, a mystery to himself, misunderstood by others, too introspective, afraid to put his best foot forward, a dreamer instead of a doer.

THE CYCLE OF SUPERMAN: 8-9-10-1 1-22 The Digit 8

POSITIVE—A balancer of spiritual and material things, the big business man, who puts inspirational ideas into concrete, or any other building material which he may be using. An 8 is the large executive who uses tact, diplomacy, co-operation, keen discrimination and an intelligent driving force to bring his business, art or commercial affairs to a successful conclusion. He is an engineer of large projects, an investor of funds for others, a leader in financial circles, a wielder of power and influence.

REVERSE—One who uses his social position, power or money for selfish purposes, a merciless driver, money-mad, supercritical, unappreciative, unaccommodating, un feeling, inviting his own ruin and disaster.

NEGATIVE—Unlucky, apparent victim of Circumstance, unsuccessful in business, investments or social ventures, due mainly to his own selfish nature. An 8 has reached the plane of superman, where he must think of others as well as himself. Until he acts constructively for the good of all he will continue to meet with adversity.

The Digit 9

POSITIVE—Lovers of all humanity, expressing in a large way their splendid artistic talents. Both money and love come to the 9 who sets into operation a positive current of good-will, sympathy and helpfulness toward everyone he meets.

<u>Money and Love</u>

46557 3645

27   18

9   9

He has a strong emotional nature; broad sympathies and an intelligent understanding of others' needs and wants. He should not be satisfied with mediocre success; the world is his field of expression. Many inspirational writers, artists, healers, humanitarian workers and world travelers are found in the 9 vibration.

REVERSE—Selfish, miserly, sarcastic, critical, arousing destructive passions in others, "trying to get something for nothing by playing on another's sympathy, fear or unsuspecting mental attitude."

NEGATIVE—One who gives everything away, whose heart rules

his head, too sympathetic for own good, used by others to further their ends.

The Number 10

POSITIVE—Same as 1, with the addition of authority, completeness and a larger viewpoint. The lessons learned in his transit through the 9 vibrations have given the individual a greater understanding of life, more sympathy with the shortcomings of others and more confidence in his own creative powers. A person whose name totals 10 can get the viewpoint of anyone with whom he may be talking if he makes his own *mind receptive at the time.

REVERSE—Same as reverse 1—arrogant, covetous, grad-tier of selfish ambition, irrespective of cost to others.

NEGATIVE—Dependent, lazy, one who starves in the midst of plenty.

The Number 11

POSITIVE—Inspiration. Enthusiastic, dynamic promoter of the higher truths. An 11 in the name indicates that the individual is an old soul, one who has come to il42

lumine the way for others less developed. The wealth of wisdom stored within his subconscious mind makes him psychic, sensitive to atmosphere, environment and personalities, full of original ideas which must be given out if he does not wish his own strong force to revert disastrously upon him. An 11 should work with the public in a large way, as a lecturer, writer, teacher, preacher or promoter.

REVERSE—Debauched, miserly, degraded. Promoters of diabolical schemes and nefarious practices.

NEGATIVE—Lacking in self-esteem, no faith in anything, unaware of their own powers, or so spiritually minded and impractical that they are forced to rely upon others for their financial support.

The Number 22

POSITIVE-4 master on all planes—making inspirational things practical. One who by use of the higher laws has become absolute master of his own environment and is thereby fitted to give wise counsel to others. Great executives, diplomats, corporation heads, statesmen and promoters of humanitarian projects on a large scale are examples of the progressive 22, while bookkeepers, clerks and office managers who abound in this vibration are those who are not aware of their large potential powers.

REVERSE—Promoters of get-rich-quick schemes, big talkers and small doers, deceitful, vain, proud, arch-criminals.

NEGATIVE—Lazy and selfish, allowing their own strong force to revert to a 4, which puts them in a limited environment, forced to take orders from others when they should be holding the reins themselves.

CHAPTER VI

YOUR NAME REVEALS YOUR PAST

ENLARGED family portraits on the parlor wall are now a dim recollection to most of us, but if you would like a glimpse of your former self, set out your name and view yourself through numbers.

Your original full name, impressed by your soul upon the minds of those about you at the time you came to earth, registers your stage of growth and development in previous lifetimes. It is a picture of You from the past, revealing your latent powers and true nature.

Setting out the original name of a prominent world figure, we have:

$$6 \quad + \quad 7 \quad + \quad 3 \quad = 16=(7) \text{ - Soul —}$$
$$\overline{16} \qquad \overline{21} \qquad\qquad \text{talents.}$$

Vowels:	6	1 9 6	6 5 5 5
	J O H N	D A V I S O N	R O C K E F E L L E R
Conso-	1 8 5	4 4 1 5	9 3 2 6 3 3 9
nants:	$\overline{14}$	$\overline{14}$	$\overline{35}$
	5	5	8

$$= 18=(9)—\text{Body—}$$
personality.

Full name:	1 6 8 5	4 1 4 9 1 6 5	9 6 3 5 6 5 3 3 5 9
	$\overline{20}$	$\overline{30}$	$\overline{56}$
	2	3	1 1

$$\overline{5} \qquad\qquad = (5\text{-}11)\text{- Mind —}$$
destiny

11 being a master number, we do not reduce it to 2 but add the remaining digits, making the total 5-11.

Soul—Natural Talents (Vowels)

The vowels of your original full name reveal your natural talents. They represent your soul or subconscious mind, in which is stored the record of your past achievements, giving a natural desire to repeat your success in such lines now.

The vowels in the above name, 6-7-3, which total 16 and then 7, indicate that in a previous lifetime Mr. Rockefeller was undoubtedly a .lover of nature (7), active in the field of finance (7).

The 6, which is also the first vowel, indicating the domestic "type," shows that he had learned to assume responsibility graciously, that he could talk (6) or keep silent (7). The 3 tells us that he was an ambitious soul, with an appreciation of the beautiful in all things and a saving sense of humor. The 7 total shows self-confidence, a firm, positive will and the determination to see everything through to the finish. His love of nature (7), still evident in Mr. Rockefeller's fondness for golf, developed a keen intuition, an inner religious nature and a desire for supreme authority in his own particular realm.

Body—Personality (Consonants)

The consonants of your original name represent your body—the materialized form of all your previous thinking. They reveal your personality or the impression you make upon others.

The consonants in the above name are 5-5-8, which total 18 or 9. 5 and 8 are two of the strongest physical numbers, indicating that Mr. Rockefeller was endowed with a good physical constitution. The two 5s made him a good judge of human nature, amiable and adaptable, the 8 gave him diplomacy, tact and driving force, while the 9 bestowed a strong and pleasing personality, able to attract those things which he desired.

Mind. (Full Name)

Your original full name shows the intellect with which you came.

The 2 of John indicates that Mr. Rockefeller had learn-ed how to collect ideas, materials and people and handle them in a systematic, tactful manner. The 3 of Davison shows ability to give complete expression to his own idea without any outside assistance.

The 11 surname shows Mr. Rockefeller to be an old soul, one who has previously achieved mastery of certain spiritual truths and who has come now to act in a larger, more universal capacity.

The total name vibration shows through the 5 that Mr. Rockefeller is a born investigator, interested in life from every angle, a splendid judge of human nature. These qualities coupled with the dynamic 11 make him a master salesman and promoter of new and advanced ideas, able to sell his products or schemes, whatever they may be, with agility and speed. The 11 gives him many inspirational ideas, far in advance of the present moment, and endows him with that psychic sense or bird's-eye view which "gets him there" ahead of time.

CHAPTER VII

YOUR PRESENT PHOTOGRAPH

YOU ARE what your name signifies. The world accepts you at your name value, your usual signature being a complete picture of yourself at the present moment.

Notwithstanding your youth and inexperience, you are older, more enduring and a far greater achievement than the Egyptian pyramids, the greatest example of perfection in the material world. Perfection of any kind is shown by a reflection of the trinity (triangle) in some form. In the pyramid, built on a square foundation, with its sides made up of 4 equilateral triangles joined at the top, we have the trinity reflected 4 times.

You, like the pyramids, are built on a square—soul (vowels), body (consonants), mind (full name) and spirit (birth path), while the triangles or trinities of numbers present in your name (1-2-3, 1-5-7, 2-4-8, 3-6-9, 8-9-10, 8-9-11, 9-10-22, 9-11-22) register your achievement in complete expression on the various planes.

As the pyramids with their 4 triangles (4X3), the 12 months of the year and the 12 signs of the zodiac all re-present numerical completion, so there are 12 points by which we gauge your intelligence, bearing and inner nature.

1. Your Type (First Vowel)

The first vowel of your name, modified by any preceding consonants, reveals your type. It is the pivotal center of your subconscious mind, indicating your dominant reaction toward life.

Using the signature by which Mr. Rockefeller has been known for many years, we have:

```
        6        +        3      =(9)--Soul—subcon-
                          21              scious desire.
Vowels:     6          6   5 5  5
          JOHN   D.   ROCKEFELLER
Consonants: 1 8 5   4   9 3 2 6 3 3 9
            1 4           3 5
            5  +  4   +    8    =17 (8)—Body—personality.
Full name: 1 6 8 5  4   9 6 3 2 5 6 5 3 3 5 9
           2 0             5 6
             2    4         11
                6                =(6-11)  Intellect and
                                         present plane
                                         of action.
```

The first vowel in the above name is "o" (6), modified by the preceding consonant "J" (1). Thus Mr. Rockefeller would be interested in those things which pertain to business, home, education and human betterment (6), but he would want to carry out his activities in such lines in his own individual (1) way.

2. Subconscious Desire (Total Vowels)

The vowels of your present signature reveal your subconscious desires.

Mr. Rockefeller has in the vowels of his present name the trinity of complete expression, 6-3-9, showing that in whatever field he chose to function he would be able to put his ideas over in a convincing manner. The 6 gives him a love of home, business and educational projects, the 3 a desire for individual self-expression, the 9 an interest in world affairs.

It is interesting to note that the medium through which Mr. Rockefeller achieved wealth and fame is made up of the same vibrations as the vowels of his name:

```
6  9              —15=(6)
O  I  L
      3           —(3)

6  9  3
   18
    9             —(9)
```

Mr. Rockefeller found in oil the very thing which he desired and which his subconscious mind knew just how to handle. This may account in some measure for his phenomenal success and for the money which followed.

Money

4 6 5 5 7

27

9

3. Personality (Consonants)

Your consonants reveal your personality, the impression you make upon others.

The consonants in the above name are 5-4-8. The 5 makes for geniality, an investigative nature, 'bye of variety and new experiences. 4 exercises a somewhat counter in-fluence, setting into operation a strong current of economy, thrift, practicality, proof and a conscientious performance of duty. The total of 8 shows a strong personality, executive ability, tact and an intelligent driving power with which to carry his ideas to a successful conclusion.

4. "Stock in Trade" (Surname)

Just as one man starting in business would handle hard-ware, another merchandise and another be a promoter of plays, so does your surname denote the materials with which you came.

The 11 of Rockefeller shows a universal, big idea, and the necessity of dealing with the public in a large way. As a capitalist Mr. Rockefeller is working in his own vibration.

Capitalist

3 1 7 9 2 1 3 9 1 2

38 / 11

5. "Modus Operandi" (Given Names or Initials)

Your given name, or the initials which you are using, show the manner in which you are handling the "materials" of your surname.

The 2 of John shows system (2) in the collection (2) of ideas (11), materials, statistics and information from all corners of the earth with which to build (4) a more efficient, economical and mechanically perfect system of big business. The 4 enables him to detect the leaks, to be observant of the necessary detail, to live, work and give in a regular manner, exercising keen discrimination, good judgment and reasoning qualities.

2 plus 4 is 6, indicating that he will use his inspirational ideas (11) in business, home and educational avenues.

6. Present Plane of Action (Signature Total)

Your total signature shows your intellect and present plane of action.

6 is usually a conservative business man, but when we link it with the dynamic 11 we have truly a master mind, who will project inspiration and enthusiasm into business, educational and human betterment lines, attracting a reflex of new and larger ideas, to be again sent forth to all mankind.

While Mr. Rockefeller's fame is linked with oil, which has the same vibrations as the vowels of his name, he put himself in still greater harmony with the universal forces by operating under the name of the Standard Oil Company:

$$
\begin{array}{ccc}
\underset{\text{1 2 1 5 4 1 9 4}}{\textbf{S T A N D A R D}} & \underset{\text{6 9 3}}{\textbf{O I L}} & \underset{\text{3 6 4 7 1 5 7}}{\textbf{C O M P A N Y}} \\[4pt]
\underline{27} & \underline{18} & \underline{33} \\[2pt]
9 \quad + & 9 \quad + & 6 \quad = 24 = (6).
\end{array}
$$

His business name carried the same total vibration as his own signature (6-11). Through promoting (11) a medium of the same vibration as his vowels under a business name vibrating the same as his own signature, he came "into his own" as a capitalist (11).

7. Planes of Expression (Nature—Man—Superman)

The three planes of expression on which man functions at the present time are: Nature (1-2-3) or the physical, Man (4-5-6-7) or the mental, and Superman (8-9-1011-22) or the spiritual.

To find on what plane the individual is most active, set out the digits in their order and place under each one the number of times such digit occurs in the name, using an x to indicate the individual or full name totals.

We are showing the letter values of Mr. Rockefeller's name below. The complete chart at the beginning of this chapter will give you the individual and full name totals.

	JOHN	D.	ROCKEFELLER	
	1 6 8 5	4	9 6 3 2 5 6 5 3 3 5 9	
	Nature		*Man*	*Superman*
x =Totals	1 2 3	4 5 6 7	8 9 11 22	
Vowel "	x	x	x	
Cons. "	1 1 3	1x 4x 3	1xx 2	
Name "	x	x x	yx	
	5	8	3	*= 16 letters
	xx	xxxxx	xxxxx 1+6=(7) keynote	

We find that Mr. Rockefeller is active on all three planes, with an even number of total digits on the planes of Man and Superman.

This shows a well-balanced individual, able to make his inspirational ideas practical.

8. Keynote (Number of Letters in Name)

Your keynote or present groove of thinking is shown by the number of letters in your name.

There are 16 letters in the above name, showing Mr. Rockefeller's interest in finance (7) and his strong love of nature (7).

9. Temperament (Odd or Even Numbers)

"A predominance of odd digits shows an emotional, inspirational nature which rebels at discipline and routine. Such a soul wants plenty of room to carry out its own ideas in its own way and finds joy in self-expression through art or humanitarian lines.

"Even digits show a practical, reasoning, methodical, constructive, executive mind, able to build, imitate and polish the creative ideas of the odd digits and make their dreams concrete realities." ("The Science of Numerology"—Author.)

1 is considered neither odd nor even.

In the above name there are 6 even numbers, 9 odd, and one 1.

While Mr. Rockefeller has more odd digits than even, there are a sufficient number of the latter to ,give him a good balance and to allow his spiritual qualities of inspiration and intuition to take the lead. His original name being 5-11, both odd numbers, and his original vowel vibration 7, also odd, it is important for him to have a predominance of odd digits in his name; otherwise his cold reasoning faculties would kill his inspirations and good intentions.

10. Dominant Traits (Predominating Digits)

Your predominating digits show characteristics of corresponding nature, while the total absence of any vibration indicates that such qualities should be developed.

If you have many more 5s in your name than any other number you are of an investigative nature, a lover of travel and variety, a good judge of human nature, interested in psychology, metaphysics and the occult, ever searching for more knowledge and a new experience.

Mr. Rockefeller has four 5s in his name, showing his breadth of view and his keen zest in life, which will keep him forever young. The three 3s, three 6s and two 9s all show wonderful ability in the expression of his big idea, with interest in health, education, domestic and world affairs.

11. Complete Individual Expression (Trinities)

Complete individual expression, or the ability to carry out your own ideas without assistance from others, is shown by the trinities in your name.

In order to put over any project successfully you must have the creative ability and aggressiveness of 1, the power of collection of 2,—whether it be of materials or people, —and the ability to express your idea in complete form, the attribute of the 3 vibration. If you are lacking in one of these three primary elements of success you will be forced to call upon someone else to supply the missing link. If you are going into business for yourself you should have one of the following trinities present in the total digits of your name:

1-2-3 (create, collect, express)—Balanced expression on the material plane in those things which make for health, comfort, pleasure, beauty and self-satisfaction. (On the higher planes 1 is found in 10 and 11, 2 in 476-8-22, 3 in 6 and 9.)

10-8-9, 11-8-9, 10-22-9, 1 1 -22-9—Balanced expression on the high plane, assuring success with the public in any line harmonious with your birth path.

Other trinities which will give you power along certain lines are:

1-5-7 (start, investigate, finish)—Science and philosophy. These numbers show strong intuitive faculties and interest in scientific, philosophical and metaphysical research. They are character analysts, philosophers, teachers, preachers and scientists.

2-4-6-8 (collect, build, maintain, operate)—Business) manufacturing, engineering and dramatic art. These give intellectual and analytical qualities with strong materialistic tendencies.

3-6-9—Creative expression in art, literature or humanitarian fields. These show a strong emotional nature, with enthusiasm and inspiration characterizing their efforts.

In the chart of Mr. Rockefeller's name shown at the beginning of this chapter we find a vowel total of 9, a consonant of 8, with 11 in the full name, giving a trinity of complete individual expression on the plane of Superman. The 11 shows a mind full of inspirational ideas, the 8 a strong personality with which to build them into form, while the 9 gives an inner understanding of just how to express his idea in the most complete, artistic manner. Such a trinity is a guaranty of large success to anyone who conscientiously lives up to such vibrations.

Noting the particular lines in which his powers will be most apt to find expression, we find in the individual and full name totals the complete business trinity of 2-46-8, while the vowels show a third3 6-9, complete expression in art, education and humanitarian avenues. Three trinities!—complete expression on three planes —a wonderful name, which cannot possibly escape success if the individual plays up to his own forces.

12. Self-Esteem and Balance

The vowels in your name indicate your self-esteem, your real selfvalue. This does not mean egotism, but the true gauge of your inner powers.

If your vowels and consonants are the same in value, there is a perfect balance between your inner and outer self. You are what you appear to be.

If your vowels are lower than your consonants, you have personality,—you enjoy helping others but take a back seat yourself. Build up your self-esteem and your health will improve accordingly.

If your vowels are higher than your consonants, you have the knowledge. Build up your personality and make people like you.

The vowels in Mr. Rockefeller's name total 9, his consonants 8, a strong number on the same plane. The 9 shows plenty of selfesteem, yet we know that it will temper his sense of justice (8) with sympathy "and kindliness.

The total of 6-11 throws all of his final digits—vowels, consonants and full name—on the high plane, showing a powerful name, able to express his ideas in a universal, masterful manner.

Comparing Mr. Rockefeller's present signature with his original name we find that he is a much bigger man than when he came. His original vowel vibration of 7 has been raised to 9, showing a growth from individual ambition to interest in world affairs. His original name totaled 5-11, his present signature is 6-11, showing that he has become more stable, more dependable, that he has developed more interest in human affairs, and now stands like the rock of Gibraltar, impervious to the winds of fate or the tide of public opinion.

CHAPTER VIII

YOUR DESTINY

THE destiny which you have come to fulfill is shown by the total digit of your original full name. To reach this goal successfully you must learn the lesson of your birth path and incorporate the spirit of its vibration into all of your activities. Your life picture is not complete without the square of soul, body, mind and spirit, or your past, present and ultimate goal, revealed in the total digits of name and birth date.

Take a former world leader, U.S. President Calvin Coolidge:

```
                       1    +         8      =(9)—Soul—
                      ‾1‾0‾           ‾2‾6‾          talents.
Vowels:           1     9        6 6   9      5
                  C A L V I N    C O O L I D G E
Consonants:   3     3 4    5     3     3   4 7
                      ‾1‾5‾            ‾1‾7‾
                       6    +          8       =14=(5)—Body—
                                                     personality.
Full name:    3 1 3 4 9 5    3 6 6 3 9 4 7 5
                       25             43
                      ‾‾7‾  +        ‾‾7‾      =14=(5)—Mind—
                                                     destiny.
Birth date:   July 4 — 1872 (1+8+7+2=18=(9)
                 7  4        18
                ‾1‾1‾       ‾9‾            =(11-9)—Spirit—life lesson
                                                     —vocation.
```

Here the month added to the day is considered 11, but the day is never added to the year in order to obtain a master number (11 or 22). Had the above birth date been September 4, in a year which totaled 7, we would have had the digits 9-4-7, totaling 20 or 2.

The vowels in the above name are higher than the consonants, showing more power than might at first appear.

They give a strong inner nature—complete individual ex-pression on the high plane 10-8-9. President Coolidge knows how to achieve his desires without becoming unduly excited; he has within himself all the qualities needed to create, execute and express his ideas on a large scale.

The 5 personality made up of 6 and 8 shows geniality, a love of home, executive qualities and a philosophical outlook on life.

The two 7s in the full name tell us that here is an individual with courage and a firm, positive will, one who will see everything' through to the finish. He can be most gracious and affable when he so desires, yet well does he keep his own counsel and the confidence of others. These 7s account for his reputation as "Silent Cal."

"Silent Cal"

193552 313

25/7   7

The 5 mind and destiny shows that in spite of the two 7s in his name Mr. Coolidge has an investigative mind, with breadth of view and a tolerance of the opinions of others. He has come not only to work out greater freedom of thought and action for himself but to be a power (5) in the line of his birth-path (11-9), an able (11) leader (9) promoting (11) the spirit of universal brotherhood (9).

Your Country

Your destiny is linked with the country in which you live. The very atmosphere is permeated with the dominant vibrations, hopes and desires which gave it birth.

How the great law of vibration operates to control the destinies of
nations and individuals, producing leaders who really represent the
desires of the people and who are in harmony with the country
itself, is revealed by the number vibrations of the U. S. A. and a few
of its Presidents.

$$
\begin{array}{ccc}
\textbf{U.} & \textbf{S.} & \textbf{A.} \\
\textbf{3} & \textbf{1} & \textbf{1} \\
\hline
& 5 &
\end{array}
$$

$$
\begin{array}{l}
8 \\
\overline{17} \qquad\qquad 6 \qquad =14=(5)\text{—Soul—} \\
\overline{3\ \ 9\ \ 5} \qquad \overline{1\ \ 5} \qquad\qquad \text{desire.} \\
\text{U N I T E D} \quad \text{S T A T E S} \\
5\ \ 2\ \ \ \ 4\ \ \ \ 1\ 2\ \ \ \ 2\ \ \ 1 \\
\hline
11 \qquad\qquad 6 \qquad =(11\text{-}6)\text{—Body—} \\
\qquad\qquad\qquad\qquad\qquad \text{personality.} \\
3\ 5\ 9\ 2\ 5\ 4 \quad 1\ 2\ 1\ 2\ 5\ 1 \\
\hline
28 \qquad\qquad 12 \\
\hline
1\emptyset \quad + \quad 3 \qquad = (4)\text{—Destiny.} \\
\end{array}
$$

Birth date: July 4 1776
$$
\begin{array}{ll}
\ \ 7\ \ 4 & \ \ 21 \\
\hline
\ \ 11 & \ \ 3 = (11\text{-}3)\text{—Spirit—} \ \mathit{5} \\
& \qquad \text{work.}
\end{array}
$$

$$
\begin{array}{l}
7 \qquad\qquad =(7)\text{—Soul—desire.} \\
\overline{10} \\
\hline
1\quad 5\quad\ \ 9\quad\ \ 1 \\
\text{A\ M\ E\ R\ I\ C\ A} \\
4\quad\ \ 9\quad\ 3 \\
\hline
16 \\
\hline
7 \qquad =(7)\text{—Body—personality.} \\
1\ \ 4\ \ 5\ \ 9\ 9\ 3\ 1 \\
\hline
32 \\
\hline
5 \qquad = 5 \text{—Destiny.}
\end{array}
$$

When the pioneers of this country decided to form a government
of their own they plainly showed their desire for freedom of
thought and action in the name they chose, the vowels of which

total 5. Their faith in this particular continent as the fruition of their dreams is found in the total of America, 5, while the abbreviation of the whole name to U. S. A. further accentuates its life-giving qualities and the varied opportunities within its borders. The Declaration of Independence was signed on July 4th, 1776, an 11-3 day. In earlier chapters we found that 3 stands for complete expression, 1 representing the father, 2 the mother and 3 the child, while 11 is a universal number. The joint vibration of 11-3 shows the birth of a new country, a child on the high plane of 11, one who has come to be an inspirational leader in the promotion of the highest ideals and a joy-bringer to all the world in lines of human betterment.

The strong personality vibration of 11-6 shows this to be a country of big business, large educational and health projects, with the home idea enlarged to include many philanthropic institutions.

The 4 destiny made up of 1 and 3 shows strength and substantiality. Through the exercise of economy and thrift, through the promotion of education and the development of individual self-expression among its citizens, it has laid the cornerstone of an enduring civilization upon which future generations can build with safety.

The destiny of the United States as shown by its 4 vibration was aptly portrayed in the words of President Coolidge himself in an address before the "Business Organization of the Budget," January 30, 1926. Speaking to cabinet officers, department chiefs and thousands of government employees, gathered to consider new economies in government, he told of the great strides in constructive economy since 1921, and how by systematic, concentrated effort the national debt had been reduced over $3,000,000,000, with a yearly saving of $170,000,000 in interest alone. He said in part:

"The spirit of real constructive economy (4) does not contemplate curtailing ample supplies for worthy purposes and real needs, but it is the enemy of waste and the ally of orderly procedure (4).

"It is not only the method by which we have built (4) railroads, developed agriculture, created commerce and established industry, . . . but it is also the method by which we have founded schools, endowed hospitals and erected places of religious worship.

"It has given to the average American a breadth of out-look (5), a variety of experience (5) and a richness of life that in former generations was beyond the reach of even the most powerful princes."

The destiny of the United States (4) added to that of America (5) gives 9—universal brotherhood. The United States is the torchbearer of peace and progress to all mankind.

The U. S. A. and the 5 Vibration

"Like attracts like" is a law of which we have often heard. The principle is to be observed in the history of nations as well as of individuals, the great law seeking to unite all things of harmonious vibrations.

There is always mutual sympathy and a common desire between those of the same vowel vibration. George Washington had the same longing for freedom as the country for which he fought, the vowels of his name and those of the United States both having a total of 5, while America indeed was the land of his heart's desire, expressing in its total digits his own vowel vibration of $7+7=14=5$.

Washington was inaugurated on April 30, 1789, a 5 day (4+-3-1714=--5).

The author of the Declaration of Independence and the statute for religious liberty in Virginia, the founder of the University of Virginia, Secretary of State in Washington's Cabinet and third

President of the United States,—Thomas Jefferson,—had the same vowel vibration as his illustrious predecessor: 7+7=14=5.

The greatest exponent of freedom in the last century was Abraham Lincoln, whose birth date was February 12, 1809 (2+3+9=14=5), a 5 day.

Theodore Roosevelt, an outstanding figure in recent years, was a 5 in both surname and destiny. He was inaugurated on September 14, 1901 (9-5-11), a 5-11 day.

Woodrow Wilson was a 5 from many angles, as may be seen by the chart of his name in Chapter XV.

Mr. Coolidge with his 5 personality and his name of 7+7=14=5 should be able to satisfy the people of this country with his administration as he is by nature what they desire.

Calvin Coolidge and the U. S. A.

When Mr. Coolidge became President he gained the universal leadership vibrations which his birth path shows he came to attain. Setting out the name by which he is now most generally known, we have:

```
                      10         +       8      =(9)—Soul—
                      19                26       subconscious desire.
Vowels;               5   9   5       6 6   9       5
                    PRES I DENT  COOL I DGE
Consonants:         7 9  1  4   5 2   3     3    4 7
                        28                26
                        19         +      8      =(9)—Body—
                                                   personality.
Full name:          7 9 5 1 9 4 5 5 2   3 6 6 3 9 4 7 5
                        4 7                 4 3
                        11         +      7      =(11·7)—Mind—
                                                   present plane
                                                   of action.
```

The total digit of. our original name is considered our destiny vibration. When we change our signature in any manner the total indicates our present plane of action. The double trinity of 1-8-9 in the above name, in both vowels and consonants, shows not only a wonderful inner power but a large growth in personality. There is now a perfect balance between the inner and the outer self. No wonder that President Coolidge can sit calmly at home in powerful poise, attending to his own affairs, while other politicians are pacing the country loudly proclaiming their wares.

While his original 5 destiny gave him an investigative mind, willing to view all sides of a question with impartiality, the present total of 11-7 shows him to be a man with an indomitable will, absolutely immovable when once his course has been decided.

Mr. Coolidge's birthday was on July 4, 1872, an 11-9 day. The birthday of the United States was on July 4, 1776, an 11-3 day. While not identical, there is perfect harmony.

Mr. Coolidge's Presidency was governed by the digit of his day (4), which controls from 27 to 54 years of age. He used his knowledge of economy, thrift, business and system in some executive capacity.

As the engineer of the affairs of the United States, he operated in harmony with the universal forces, bringing economy and all the substantial 4 virtues into play in the upbuilding of the United States, helping it to fulfill its 4 destiny.

The addition of President (11) to his full name (5) makes his total name vibration 5-11, showing that he was now master (11) of his own destiny (5).

CHAPTER IX

WHAT DOES THE FUTURE HOLD?

YOUR present earth experience will always be colored by the total digit of your birth, yet within this large span your life moves in cycles of greater or less degree from beginning to infinity. Each year brings certain influences to bear upon you and your environment which it would be well to note if you desire to prosper. Regulating your activities in accord with the year's vibrations eliminates cross-currents and establishes you harmoniously with the universal stream of progress.

27-Year Cycles

Your life is divided into three large periods, governed by the digits of your birth path, during which time you should cultivate the qualities and engage in the activities which such vibration indicates.

The digit of your month controls from 1 through 27 years of age.

The digit of your day governs from 27 through 54. The digit of your year is the controlling vibration from 54 on.

While the total digit of your birth should always be given paramount consideration, the sooner you learn the lessons of its respective digits, the sooner will you pass from your month into your day and from your day into your year, arriving at your ultimate goal much quicker than if you meekly await your turn at the close of the cycle.

9-Year Cycles

Each letter of your given names controls a period of 9 years. When you have passed through these once you return and begin again with the first letter.

Within these cycles are smaller ones, governed in length by your predominant digit, each one being marked at its close by some important event.

Setting out the given name of President Coolidge and noting the 9year cycles controlled by the various letters, we have:

54-63	63-72	72-81	81-90	90-99		
1-9	9-18	18-27	27-36	36-45	45-54	
C	A	L	V	I	N	
3	1	3	4	9	5	

In the life of President Coolidge the 7 vibration plays an important part, it being the total digit of Calvin, of Coolidge, and the month of his birth.

Mr. Coolidge began the practice of law in 1897 ($1+8+9+7=25=7$), a 7 year, when 25 years of age, in a year cycle of 7 ($2+5=7$) within the 9-year cycle of "L" or 3. Having finished (7) his education, he was now able to enjoy complete individual self-expression (3) in his chosen profession. It was a most auspicious time in which to begin his career as a lawyer (3).

He was married October 4, 1905, on an 11 day, in his 34th year, the digit of his age ($3+4$) being 7 in a 9-year period governed by "V" or 4, which influence called for the exercise of intellectual acumen and the exercise of economy, thrift, regularity and conscientious application to duty.

His terms as Governor of Massachusetts in 1919 and 1920 and as President of the United States have both fallen within the cycle of "N," governed by 5, his destiny number.

He was inaugurated on August 3, 1923, in the early part of his 52nd year ($5 + 2\ 7$) in a one year cycle of 7 in the larger one of 5 just noted above.

Mr. Coolidge will be 54 on July 4, 1926, when he will return again to the -first—letter -of his name and come under the influence of 3, giving him an opportunity to express his own individual ideas through humanitarian channels and enjoy life to the full.

The birthday of President Coolidge being July 4, 1872 (7-4-9), the first 27 years of his life were controlled by the 7 of his month, during which time he was perfecting (7) his education and starting in business for himself—which should be the object of everyone with such a vibration.

The period of his life just now closing has been con-trolled by the 4 of his day. During the last 9 years of this cycle he has been particularly active in using his intellectual keenness and executive ability in the exercise of constructive economy in state and national affairs. His term as President of the United States (4) at this time seems particularly opportune. He exemplifies in splendid measure the sterling qualities of the 4 vibration for which our government stands.

Beginning with his 54th birthday Mr. Coolidge will come under the 9 vibration of his year, when new occasions for world travel and large humanitarian problems will present themselves for his consideration. This will give him the opportunity to fulfill his mission in life (11-9)

shown by his total birth path digit—and be an inspirational (11) leader in promoting (11) a world brotherhood (911) .

Yearly Influences

Within the larger cycles each year brings you its own particular lessons. Among the first to be considered is the general aspect of the year itself, found by adding its digits.

1926   is 1-9-2-6, totaling 18 or 9—a good love year, one in which the spirit of universal brotherhood will engage the attention of the world (9). Bonds (9) should be a good investment. You should finish up all past experiences, bless them, send out good-will to everyone, and prepare a clean slate for next year's adventure.

1927   is 1-9-2-7, totaling 19-10 or 1—a splendid year in which to make that contemplated change, promote some new enterprise, place a new invention upon the market or add another line to your present operations. Aviation will receive a new impetus. This is a period in which you must stand firmly on your own feet, discard the advice of others and listen carefully to your own intuition, exercising initiative and aggressiveness at all times. You cannot afford to be lazy in a 1 year; if you are, someone is apt to step on you. Wake up to your real possibilities!

1928   is 1-9-2-8, totaling 20 or 2. This is the time to collect materials, statistics, information—systematize it and build your idea into concrete form, ready for public approval the coming year. Exercise patience and tact in all your dealings. You cannot afford to be angry this year. Develop a hobby, study dramatic art, build, maintain and operate, but leave the promotion of any new enterprise until such time as an odd vibration controls.

1929   is 1-9-2-9, totaling 21 or 3. Behold the women, prominent in politics and in all high places! This is the year when the men should plan to take that long deferred vacation. Art, beauty, health and humanitarian programs will be the order of the day. Life will take on a new ex-pression, with the women holding sway.

1930   is 1-9-3-0, totaling 13 or 4. This year will mark substantial building progress in all lines, especially in education, manufacturing and commercial affairs. If you wish to be in harmony with the universal forces you must attune your life to regularity in work, play, living and giving, exercising economy, thrift, discrimination, leaving nothing undone to accomplish your ends. Next year you'll have time to travel.

1931   is 1-9-3-1, totaling 14 or 5. This year will see relief from the strenuosity of 1930. You may spend your summer in the Rockies and winter in Florida if you stayed on the job last year. But before you go, be sure your affairs are in perfect order, as all people, policies and pro-grams will be subject to investigation. All hidden corners will be thoroughly searched and detectives will find their business thriving. Psychology , metaphysics, vocational guidance, will be popular subjects of discussion, while "How to stay forever young" will be the paramount theme of the day. This is the time to investigate your prospects among the opposite sex, as next year you may want to settle down.

1932   is 1-9-3-2, totaling 15 or 6. A splendid year to invest in a wedding ring, build a home and establish yourself in domesticity. Business will be active, with educational and health programs prominent in the daily press. It is a period in which you must assume responsibility graciously if you wish to grow. And don't forget to smile, whether you feel like it or not, for the blues are taboo in 1932.

1933   is 1933, totaling 16 or 7. Now is the time to enter the field of finance, go into business for yourself, or bring yourself to the country and engage in agriculture.

Take things easy as much as you can, reserving some time each day for quiet meditation, allowing your intuition to lead the way. Bring everything you do to ultimate perfection, keep every engagement on the dot, talk little, think much, and you will be able to "cash in" on your ideas in 1934.

1934   is 1-9-3-4, totaling 17 or 8—a year of prosperity, marked by forward strides in business and commercial activities, with engineering feats that startle the world. Use reason, tact and good judgment in all your affairs, keeping a perfect balance between earth and the higher realm.

Similar influences apply to the months within each year, according to their numerical order in the calendar.

1910 was the last 11 year and there will not be another until 2009, but in the month of November of every year the 11 influence will be apparent in spiritualistic and psychic phenomena, while matters of religion will be widely discussed. It is a splendid month for promotion schemes and the spread of new propaganda.

1939 is the next 22 year. This should be marked by the largest humanitarian projects which the world has ever known. Pure materialism will give way to more spiritual things, while the dreamers will become practical doers. It will be a pivotal year of great import in the history of the twentieth century.

Your Lessons This Year

There are two particular vibrations which operate upon you as an individual in each year.

The first of these is found by adding the month and day of your birth to the digit of the year. Referring to the birth date of President Coolidge, we find that July 4, 1926, has the vibrations of 7-4-9, totaling 11-9, the same as his original birthday. Therefore this should be an out-standing year for him in every way. A similar vibration of large import appeared on the date of his inauguration, August 3, 1923 (8-3-6), an 11-6 day. Adding the digit of his month and day to 1923 we have 7-4-6 or 11-6 as a prominent influence in the year 1923. It is significant that this high point in his career occurred on a day having the same vibration as his own for the year.

The second individual influence to be considered is the digit of your age. If you have passed your 27th birthday you are in your 28th year and the digit of your age is 10— a splendid time to make a new start and polish your headlight with courage.

Cycles in National Events

Nations as well as individuals move in cycles, while the nature of important events is always significantly shown in the date vibration.

Independence Day, July 4, 1776 (7-4-3), an 11-3 day, has already been mentioned in a previous chapter as de-noting the birth of a new government, or a new era of self-expression of far-reaching influence.

The first strong note in our existence as an individual nation was struck on October 19, 1781 (10 +111) + 8=1(Q) a 1 day, when at Yorktown the Colonies gained their decisive victory over the British and ended the Revolutionary War. The three is in this date throw their firm positive force in the direction of the 8, the highest physical number, showing not only the birth of the strongest nation (1) on earth, but one bound to be a promoter (1) of big business (8) throughout the world, co-operating (8) with other nations, yet always maintaining its distinctive individuality and independent (1) atmosphere.

The most important event of the present generation occurred November 11, 1918, at 11 o'clock a. m., when the Armistice was signed. 1.1 always stands for a new beginning and in this particular date, the complete triangle of 1 1 s, in a year which totals 10 (1111-11-10), shows not only the entrance of a new era, but also one of universal import, which will be marked by the most dynamic, unusual and psychic influences which the world has yet known.

CHAPTER X

BEST DAYS, COLORS and MUSICAL KEY

OUR BEST DAYS are good days for everyone, but on those days, which have the same vibration as your total birth digit the forces of the universe are especially harmonious to any new undertaking you may wish to promote.

At such times you should make a careful note of the impressions received, as events of a similar character ex-tending over a period of several weeks or months are strongly indicative of the course you should follow. If adverse conditions appear, seek out the root and cause and let your inner self reveal the secret. Strengthen your own forces by sending out a strong current of good-will to all the universe, and by the law of reflex action it is bound to return with blessings in its wake.

To find the vibration of any day, add the digits of month, day and year together, and reduce the final total. The only exception is when 11 or 22 appear and make a combination total. In such case, if your birth path be 11-4, your best days are all those which total either 11 or 4.

July 31, 1926, shows a total digit of 11-9. July is the 7th month. The digits of 31 added are 4. The digits of 1926 (1-9-2-6) total 18, while 18 (1-8) totals 9. While we never add the day or the month to the year in order to obtain an 11 or 22, when the first two digits of the date (month and day) total 11 or 22, they show the possibility of leadership in the realm of the year vibration.

August 11, 1926, shows the digits 8-11-9. Here we add the 8 and 9, which gives us 17 or 8, and allow the 11 to stand intact. This gives a total birth digit of 11-8. August 9, 1939, shows the digits 8-9-22. Here we add the 8 and 9, giving us 17 and a total digit of 8-22.

Every day can be made a winner if you live in harmony with its dominant note. You can easily form the habit of noting its value and, whenever your vibration appears, making a special effort, through the color of your dress and general activities, to tune in with the universal forces.

On a 1 day—Start something, be aggressive, act on your intuition, heed not the advice of others.

On a 2 day—Be receptive to suggestions, learn to co7 operate, try to get the other fellow's point of view, be observing, study and collect your materials for a more complete expression tomorrow.

On a 3 day—Express your own individual self in some creative way. Be happy,—make seven people smile and you will take a new lease on life.

On a 4 day—Rise early, hum a march tune, walk briskly to the office and get your mail out on schedule time. Work done well today will give you more satisfaction than any kind of a vacation.

On a 5 day—Be active and enthusiastic, investigate your business and social prospects, study human nature, analyze yourself and your surroundings and generate new pep into your environment.

On a 6 day—Look after your business interests, your health and education, and surprise your wife with a box of candy, or, better still, tell her you will stay home with. the children tonight while she goes out for a little recreation.

On a 7 day—Finish up the odds and ends, then bring yourself to the country and take things easy; listen to your "still small voice" and you will get a new idea for business tomorrow.

On an 8 day—Be a real executive, organize your forces, drive yourself and your business with justice and tact. Render a real service in a big way and you will he blessed with equally large returns,

On a 9 day—If you have any artistic talent, prepare to shine today in some public performance. Send out good will to all the world; hold not a single grudge; find something in every one to commend, voicing your appreciation thereof in words. This is a love day, but you must first send out the vibration if you would have love in return. Money likewise should appear if you are generous and philanthropic in your giving.

On an 11 day—You will get an inspiration; listen to it and make a new beginning. Deal with the public, let your light shine, and give out the knowledge you have to others.

On a 22 day—Lay big plans,—the sky is your limits—but make your ideas practical. Be energetic, organize, advise, yet do not fail to keep your word, for the adverse aspect is laziness and glowing promises unfulfilled. This is the day when earth and heaven meet and the best time ever to build your dreams into concrete realities.

Colors

Color is one of the primary mediums for transmitting the characteristics of each digit to people or things. To find the vibration of any color, add the letter values of the word.

While the colors of your name can be worn attractively, those of your birth path have a much stronger and a greater health-giving influence, as they carry the vibrations you have come to develop. Choose from the colors of your birth date the one most in harmony with the digit of the day and let it play a dominant note in your dress and room furnishings.

If you are in business, feature the color of the day in your window display.

A few colors with their number vibrations are shown below:

1.   1—Crimson, flame.
2.   2—Salmon, gold.
3.   3—Rose, orchid.
4.   4—Blue, green, indigo.
5.   5—Lemon, pink.
6.   6—Scarlet, orange, heliotrope, wine, gray, henna.
7.   7—Brick, purple.
8.   8--Mauve, tan, buff, canary.
9.   9—Red, brown, taupe, lavender.

11 White, black, yellow, violet, dark green, dark blue.

22—Cream.

The same law applies to flowers, perfumes, fruits, foods, trees, gems, musical instruments or anything else in the universe. You are the magnetic center of your world, attracting "your own"—those things which have the same vibration as your date of birth being of primary importance, those of your name a close second.

Music

To cheer you on your way each digit has its tone and color. Mrs. Balliett, in "The Philosophy of Numbers," gives the musical vibration of numbers as follows:

$$\text{"C--D--E--F--G--A--B}$$
$$1 \quad 2 \quad 3 \quad 4 \quad 5 \quad 6 \quad 7$$
$$8 \quad 9$$

22 expresses the full octave of D.
11 expresses the full octave of C."

She further suggests that you make up your own life song, using the digits of your birth path as the basic motif.

You will find it relaxing to the nerves and conducive to a peaceful frame of mind.

CHAPTER XI

WHY CHANGE YOUR NAME?

YOUR name is a good one because it represents you. Do not change it unless you can make it better.

Every change in name or signature opens a new door of opportunity for progress or retrogression. If you have changed your name through marriage or otherwise, note carefully whether you have raised or lowered your vibration. Changing your name will profit you nothing if you do not really express the positive characteristics of the new vibration and live up to the standard for which it stands.

At the same time, if you have really made an inner growth through your own efforts, circumstances will automatically shape themselves to give you a corresponding name. You will be elected President (11) of your company or Grand (8) Master (22) of your lodge.

The reason why you are here is shown by your birth date. If it is higher than the digit of your original name you have some big lessons to learn. You have come to gain honor and fame and strive for wealth and glory.

If your original name contains a master number (11 or 22) you are an old soul and have come to give out the knowledge already gained and to work in some public teaching capacity, through writing, lecturing or humanitarian lines, while the smaller digits of your birth path indicate the qualities you need to develop in order to make you a more rounded personality. You should care naught for wealth or fame; your mission is to deliver the message which comes to you through your inspirational and psychic faculties.

What you really are at the present moment is revealed by your most frequent signature. It shows your present plane of action and understanding.

The only way by which you can master any lesson is by use of the mind with which you were endowed. If you are supposed to do a problem in algebra or geometry, something higher than 1-2-3--if your birth path contains 9, 11 or 22, it is plainly evident that in order to meet such problems you must have an intellect of equal capacity. Otherwise you are "up against it" and will have to do the best you can.

The most scientific method of gaining this under-standing, if you have it not, is to raise the total value of your name to that of your birth path. After you have worn this vibration long enough the meaning thereof will sink into your subconscious mind and your intuition will reveal the path to follow.

Adjustment of Your Name

1.   Your total name digit should be in harmony with that of your birth, equal or higher in value, and in the same zone.

2.   The more nearly your vowels and consonants approach each other in value, the more you are what you appear to be. Remember that your vowels reveal your inner force, your consonants your personality. Therefore you must have plenty of self-esteem (vowels) if you would really make a strong impression (consonants) upon others. The higher your vowels the greater your inspiration, as a general rule; the higher your consonants, the greater your influence over other people; yet there should be a reasonable balance between the two if you wish to be a well poised individual.

3.   In changing your name it is well to keep the total vowel vibration in the same zone with that of your original name; yet if all the digits in your birth path be even and your vowels odd, it may *be that you will have to turn yourself inside out in order to strike a perfect balance.

4.   If you wish to enter business for yourself or accomplish large things through your own efforts, you should have at least one trinity in your name showing the 1-2-3 principle—the ability to carry out your ideas without assistance from others. If you are lacking in one of these someone else will have to complete the picture and share with you the ultimate glory.

5: If you wish to specialize in some particular line, that trinity likewise should appear in your name. If your ambition be in literature or art, see that you have the trinity of complete artistic expression, 3-6-9; if psychology, sociology and personnel work engage your attention, your name should show a 1-5-7; if business success be your goal in life, 2-4-6-8 will give you the necessary building qualities, while 11 and 22 show mastership in any line.

Your Original Name an Index to Your True Nature No matter how you may change your name, your original nature will always remain in the background, coloring your entire life. A typical example of such influence is that of Douglas Fairbanks, one of the most thrilling of movie actors. His original name, Douglas Ulmann, shows a 5 total in both vowels and consonants, with a full name of 10, while his birth date, May 23, 1883 (5+5+2= 12=-73), also contains a double 5 vibration, colored with the artistic 3. From four angles Douglas Fairbanks is a 5, twice in his original name and twice in his birth path. Throughout his career he has been a glowing example of the "go-getter" vivid, active, experiencehunting 5 vibration, yet his present name is lacking in any such digit total. The only 5 to be found is the small consonant "n," scarcely sufficient to furnish the thrills for his many-sided nature. He is one of those individuals who will always be in the lead (10) and "get there," no matter what mountains he has to climb.

Choosing a Nom de Plume

In choosing a name for a professional career, care should be taken to make it fit the particular field you intend to enter, not forgetting to harmonize it with your birth path total.

All of the digits should be present in your name in some manner if you wish to influence all classes of people. If such is not possible, then see to it that you have an 11 or a 22 and also a 1, and thereby you will include all others.

Striking examples of those who have risen to fame following a change in name would fill several volumes, two world figures being Mark Twain, the famous humorist, author of "Huckleberry Finn" and "Tom Sawyer," and Sarah Bernhardt, the most famous actress of all time.

The original name of Mark Twain was Samuel Langhorne Clemens, which had a vowel vibration of 9-3-1, totaling 4; a consonant vibration of 8-1-7, totaling 7, and a total vibration of 8-4-8, totaling 20. Not a very auspicious name for an author.

Under his pen name Mark Twain had a vowel vibration of 1-10 (11), a consonant vibration of 6-3 (9), and a total vibration of 7-22 (7-22). In his consonants he gained the complete trinity of literary and artistic ex-pression, 6-3-9, while his total digits show the trinity of balanced creative expression on the high plane 11-22-9. The 1 of his first vowel and the 22 of his last name enabled him to reach all classes, as between them are found all other vibrations. A splendid name, giving him inspiration, personality, and a big understanding of the needs of the average mind, while the strong 8 of his real nature came through with the necessary analytical qualities to make his creations real and to place a true value on their monetary worth.

Sarah Bernhardt was christened Rosine Bernard, which latter name shows a vowel vibration of 2+6, totaling 8, a consonant vibration of 6-11 and a -total vibration of 8+8=16=7. Her birth date was October 22, 1844: 10-22-8, giving a total of 22-9, the most perfect trinity of numbers possible for an actress.

In the name of Sarah Bernhardt she maintained her original vowel vibration of 2+6=8, had a consonant vibration of 9+3=12=3, and a total of 2+9_11. Here the 9 of her last name met the 9 of her birth path, giving her full and free artistic expression in a large way, while the 11 total gave her unbounded inspiration with which to sway the public mind and make her an outstanding (11) figure in the realm of dramatic (2) art (9) Her full name (11) was now on the same plane with the 22 and 9 of her birth and in harmony with both. Her powerful inner self shown by the vowel vibration of 8 gave her that eternal driving force which enabled her to conquer fate. A strong, indomitable soul she was, whose glory will not fade, and whose accomplishments were truly those of a 22-9 vibration.

CHAPTER XII

VOCATION—BUSINESS

THE total digit of your birth, with its respective digits of month, day and year, shows the character attributes that you have come to develop, which when acquired will attract the work calling for the exercise of such qualities. The sooner you make them a part of yourself, the sooner will your right work find you.

While the final digit of birth should be given para-mount consideration, the digits of month, day and year play an important part in the choice of a vocation, particularly during the periods which they govern.

Your Right Sphere

Suppose your birth date were March 1st, 1899, the digits of which are 3-1-9, totaling 13 or 4. This does not necessarily mean that you should be an office manager or an automobile mechanic, both of which vocations can be successfully handled by a 4, but it does mean that you are to develop your intellect and obtain a first-class education along the lines of music, art, law, healing or other humanitarian calling, remembering that 1 always accentuates the qualities of the other digits to which it is related.

During the first 27 years of your life, governed by the 3 vibration, you should study music, dramatic art, build up your physical constitution and engage in all kinds of activities which will develop your self-expression.

Between the age of 27 and 54 you are under the in-fluence of the 1 vibration, when you should begin to stand on your own feet, discard the advice of others and act on your own intuition. This is the time for you to do creative work, write your own compositions, organize, manage and promote your own plays, and become the brilliant com-poser or builder along artistic lines which the total of

4 enables you to be. When a 4 "delivers the goods" he builds (4) a reputation which will remain with him for-ever.

The more aggressive you are during this cycle of 1, the more "do and dare" spirit you put into your efforts, the sooner will you "arrive" in the 9 of your year,—full and free artistic expression in a universal way, with opportunity for extended travel, fame and the good things of life,—the natural reflex action from the creative efforts of your previous cycle.

Therefore, in choosing a life work take into consideration all of your birth path digits, but give preference to the grand total. If the work you do is not listed here, find Tis"---he number value of its dominant word, and see whether you have a like vibration. While there have been many famous lawyers in the professional 7, law itself totals 9, while lawyer totals 3. 3 and 9 are also the art and humanitarian numbers. With both of these digits in your birth path, look to the remaining numbers and to the original name in order to determine in which branch of self-expression you should throw your creative efforts.

A few occupations calling for the particular qualities of the different vibrations are shown in the following list of Vocations:

1., Inventor, designer, promoter, aviator, superintendent, teacher, writer or lecturer along metaphysical and occult lines—creative work in avenues indicated by other digits of the birth path or name.

2.   Statistician, secretary, collector, arbitrator, diplomat, actor.

3.   Artist, musician, lawyer, nurse, dietitian, physician, naturecure specialist, writer, entertainer, manager of hotel, restaurant or beauty parlor, salesman of advertising, drugs, art goods, musical instruments, cosmetics, groceries, artisan in any line. Happy in those avenues which make for health, beauty or comfort. Should avoid, positions calling

for too close confinement, long hours or prolonged attention to detail. Individual self-expression is absolutely essential to success.

4. A builder, either on the physical or mental plane, a mechanic, draftsman, architect, electrician, manufacturer, efficiency expert, office executive, stenographer, clerk, bookkeeper, accountant, dealer in coal, brick and building materials. Any routine business requiring a combination of intellect, skill, perseverance, endurance and energy.

5. Investigator, detective, character analyst, vocational employment director, writer on scientific, occult or metaphysical subjects, a rejuvenator on all planes—the traveling salesman, vaudeville player or noted psychology lecturer. Must have speed and action; is not happy in routine work but must have the opportunity to make his own schedule and exercise his own intuitive powers in the hand-ling of any situation.

6. The home-maker, business man, teacher, educator, writer or public speaker, hotel manager, head of hospital or other public institution, nurse, doctor, interior decorator, florist. Must he cheerful and happy in service for others in order to be successful.

7. The professional man, supreme in his own realm, one who runs his own business and has his own established center of activity, successful in law, dentistry, real estate, horticulture, agriculture, mining, or as preacher, teacher and writer. Dislikes manual labor, does best in an atmosphere of refinement and culture. Perfection, finish and quality are required rather than size or quantity.

8. Engineer, banker, broker, corporation lawyer, executive, organizer, business or corporation head,—builders on all

planes where keen discrimination, good judgment, perseverance, tact and driving qualities are needed. Also make good actors.

9.   Artist, musician, actor, physician, healer, lawyer, beauty expert, writer, lecturer, humanitarian worker, world traveler, also successful in horticulture, floriculture and landscape gardening. Must have free artistic expression in a large way.

11. Inspirational speaker or writer, lecturer, preacher, promoter, sales manager, leader in public affairs and in the lines indicated by other digits of birth path or name.

22. Executive, diplomat, arbitrator, actor, librarian, business manager, statesman, corporation lawyer, humanitarian adviser of the highest order, active in practical philanthropic projects. Often found as bookkeeper, clerk or accountant, but should realize that such occupation is the limited aspect of the 22 vibration. He should fit himself for public service, study dramatic art, public speaking, character analysis and vocational guidance and prepare himself to act in some advisory capacity in an unlimited environment.

The Proper Business Medium

Having decided to enter business for yourself, what is the next important point to be considered? The proper selling medium.

The story of John D. Rockefeller's success in oil is told in Chapter VII. There were several points of vibratory contact between his own name and his main "line." He promoted a medium having the same vibration as his vowels, while his business name and his own signature carried the same values.

Henry Ford rose to fame with the Ford car. His name totals 5, made up of 7 plus 7, totaling 14 or 5. Automobile totals 5, but when he had perfected it to the point where it deserved a name, he called it the Ford (7) car (4), which together totals 11, a master number, making it stand supreme in its own field. Mr. Ford was born on July 30, 1863, the digits of his birth path being 7-3-9, totaling 19 or 10. This shows plainly that as an inventor Mr. Ford was in his "right pew," working in a vibration identical with his name. Through adhering to his own ideas he evolved an article of superior merit, as its name reveals, while he has wooed still further the vibratory forces of large success in the business name of Ford Motor Company, which is made up of the digits 7-9-6, totaling 22, the highest vibration of all.

Location

If your name totals 22, you should do well in Boston, which has the same vibration. If your signature is only 4, Washington, D. C., would be a good location. A city whose total number value is the same as your own will be active in those lines which you are able to handle.

You must remember that before trying to adjust yourself to a location numerologically, you must first adjust your name to your birth path. You will always find opportunity for growth and development in a city having the same vibration as your date of birth. If you have a name in harmony with your birth, and then settle down in a city with a like vibration, you have two points of harmony which should make for assured success.

If you have a choice of street numbers, one which is in harmony with your present signature should control, not forgetting that your own name and business name should be odd or even, according to the digit of birth.

You should also do well in a city whose vowel vibration is the same as your total name. In such instance you are what they desire, and it is up to you to give satisfaction.

CHAPTER XIII

SELLING TIPS

NOTE : When we speak of a 1 or a 2 individual, we mean one in whom such number is the predominating digit, whether in individual or full name totals, added strength being shown if it also appears in date of birth.

SUCCESSFUL salesmanship depends on a forehand knowledge of your customer. This can easily be obtained from his business card by use of the table in Chapter III.

1.   If you are selling to a 1, an individual Whose first vowel is "a" or whose total name is 10, be sure that your article is different from the ordinary run of things. He wants something new, novel or intellectual, with distinctly progressive features.

2.   If you are selling to a 2, be sure that you are perfectly groomed before entering the "inner sanctuary.), He desires those things which will give him comfort, ease and prestige. Use tact and diplomacy in your approach, with just a touch of expert flattery, and it will help you land the order.

3.   If you are selling a 3, he enthusiastic about some-thing which makes an appeal to the eye, conveying the idea of beauty, comfort, health or pleasure. To get his name on the dotted line, invite him out to a first-class dinner but close the deal between the last two courses. If you give him time to think it over he will be apt to change his mind. 3 can also be reached through his sympathies.

4.   If you are selling a 4, make your visit short and snappy; he has no patience with social calls. Be sure your logic is sane and sound and your article worth double the money. He cares not for beauty or style; the thing he buys must be practical, workable, durable, and guaranteed to last.

5.   If you are selling a 5, breeze in with a cheerful smile and pique his curiosity. He wants to know all there is to know, so keep him guessing. Give him a brief character sketch of himself, from his face, his head, his hand or his name, and you will have his whole attention. Then with speed and agility present your topic. It must have a human appeal, afford a new experience or present some unusual departure from the regular scheme of things. He is interested in life and in .staying young; so make your attack accordingly.

6.   If you are selling a 6, one with a first vowel "o," a last name Smith, or some other form of this vibration, you must be able to hold your own in any argument. He is interested most in those things which make for beauty and comfort in his home, the better education of his children or the more efficient conduct of his business. Your article must not only be worth the money but must have an esthetic air about it, something useful, beautiful and of high quality.

7.   If you are selling a 7, be careful! He has a decided mind of his own, and of all vibrations his is the hardest to influence. Ask his advice first, get an expression from him and then counter with your idea. Present your proposition complete in every detail, dwell on its perfection, finish and quality. Never mind about the quantity; he wants the best or none at all.

8.   If you are selling an 8, he sure to radiate an atmosphere of success and prosperity yourself. He is interested in constructive things which are practical, attractive, elegant, and generous in proportions. Convince him that your idea put into practice in his business will increase his output, strengthen his finances, provide just compensation to his employees and make him an outstanding figure in his world.

9.   If you are selling a 9 and have a pleasing air about you, you will have a sympathetic listener, provided your project is sufficiently large in proportions to engage his attention. He is interested in those things which pertain to music, art and self-expression on a large scale. He is also the strong advocate of all things which make for better health, more wealth or increased enjoyment of life from every angle. Anything which has a human-interest appeal will meet with a favorable reception if you are large enough yourself to present it in world terms.

11. If you are selling an 11, you must be inspired with a big, new and wonderful idea. You must be enthusiastic, yet calm and psychic enough to get his psychic reaction to your proposition. He is interested in those things which will give him greater inspiration, more influence over other people, greater opportunity to expound his ideas, and an established place in the public eye.

22. If you are selling a 22 you must have a proposition of merit, practical as well as idealistic, combining reason with human sympathy and proof with your philosophy. Give your prospect a world view, and direct his attention to this opportunity for public service. Even though he be a bookkeeper or clerk, he knows very well that there are larger things in store for him, with international diplomacy topping the list.

CHAPTER XIV

FRIENDS AND MARRIAGE

WHY do you take an immediate liking to some individuals and feel a natural antipathy toward others? It is a matter of vibration. Just as the chemical elements of calcium and carbon have an affinity for each other and as oil and water do not mix, so do our vibrations attract similar ones and repel others.

Your Friends

Your friends are those who think as you do, feel as you do or have a like ambition.

When you meet a person with a vowel vibration the same as your own there is an immediate bond of sympathy and understanding, and the more individual vowels you have, in common, the stronger will be the attraction. Your subconscious selves have a desire for expression along the same lines which makes for real enjoyment.

One whose consonants are the same as yours will be a splendid friend for your idle hours, as the outward things of life have a kindred appeal.

One whose full name is the same or in the same trinity of expression makes a splendid business companion. Your minds register on the same plane, whether in work or study.

One whose total birth digit is the same as yours is in your present grade of school. You may have come from widely separated localities with a totally different back-ground, yet you are here now for a common purpose and should get along famously together, tackling the same problems with co-operation, sympathy and courage.

One whose name has the same vibration as your birth has something to teach you, provided he is on your mental plane. The probability is that when you meet such a person you will find that one of his birth digits is present in your name, and that you will both benefit from such association.

A strong point of contact frequently noted is where one individual is (through his total name) what the other desires (in his vowels). A person whose total vowels equal your full name will attach himself to you and remain there unshaken whether you notice him or not. You have something that he wants. After a time you become so accustomed to the situation that you begin to take it as a matter of course. If he has nothing in his name to answer your vowels or birth digit you will be doing all the giving and he all the receiving, but if his name equals your vowels, then you are complements of each other and there will be an opportunity for splendid growth through, such a friendship. Each has an inner knowledge of the other's destiny and at the same time is expressing in his full character the other's subconscious desires.

Marriage

In order to have an ideal home life there must be some harmony between the individual vibrations. Marriage itself can sometimes bring this about through the wife taking the husband's name. In addition thereto there are several ways by which the atmosphere can be made more happily harmonious.

One splendid assurance of genuine pleasure is where husband and wife have the same vowel total. With the same vibrations there are like desires; they enjoy the same things, and enjoy each other, the chief danger being that they are apt to settle down in such snug self-satisfaction that their real growth may be retarded. They should endeavor to extend their interests beyond their own family circle and continue to grow, together.

Those with the same total name vibrations can co-operate splendidly, as their minds are on the same plane and their activities can be made of a like enjoyable nature. If they are not the same but are in the same trinity, it makes for a splendid partnership, as each has the qualities which the other lacks, both being necessary for complete success.

Those with the same birth path have the same qualities of character to develop; they can succeed in similar occupations; in fact, they can go all through life together, with sympathy and tolerance for the other fellow, as they have the same shortcomings themselves. This is a very successful marriage vibration.

For those who have 11s or 22s in their original names it would appear that the law of complements should rule. They are already old souls, and if they have elsewhere a 1 in their name they are undoubtedly in their last earth cycle. Their progress may have been over different routes and hence their present lesson not the same, yet each is the ideal expression of the other's heart's desire, which makes for a most satisfying, enduring companionship. It may not have the zest in mutual accomplishment which is found when the birth paths are the same, as each now has his own particular destiny to fulfill, nor the thrill of pleasure enjoyed when the vowels are identical, yet there is an inner feeling that each is helping the other to complete his last initiation in this cycle, which unselfish efforts will eventually register in a subsequent change of name, bringing their inner desires closer together through a harmony of vowels.

Another most happy marriage relation is where each one has in his original name the birth vibrations of the other.

CHAPTER XV

TWO-MINUTE SKETCHES

From the Number of Your Sign in the Zodiac

THE characteristics of each vibration being transmitted by its digit to whatever such number applies, it naturally follows that the digit which determines the position of each sign in the zodiac will cause its particular qualities to be reflected in such sign.

Brief character sketches from an astrological standpoint are given here, showing how the two sciences of Astrology and Numerology correlate and support each other. A more complete treatment of the subject from this angle is found in "The Science of Numerology," by the author.

Number Features of the 12 Signs

1.   ARIES—March 22 to April 20. Symbol, the ram. First fire sign, governing the head and face.

This influence gives an emotional nature and the strong 1 characteristics of aggressiveness, independence, courage, push, energy, originality, determination, keen intellect and intuition. The Aries individual is a natural leader in any field, interested in psychology, metaphysics and the occult. Because of his great desire to rule he can never be driven or forced.

His adverse characteristics, common to the 1 vibration, are impatience, anger, stubbornness, selfishness, egotism, arrogance and jealousy. He should cultivate patience and concentration, avoid worry and anxiety and learn to obey the "still small voice" within.

2.   TAURUS—April 21 to May 21. Symbol, the bull.

First earth sign, governing the neck and throat.

This influence gives the individual a receptive, reserved, conservative "stay-on-the-ground" nature, with geniality, sympathy, a splendid memory and large talent in imitation. He is fond of books and reading, close-mouthed regarding own affairs, yet magnetic and well liked. Interested mainly in those things which make for the satisfaction of the senses. Has strong will (2) yet can be influenced by arousing his sympathy. Excels in literature and mathematics. Is practical and constructive in his business operations.

His 2 defects are stubbornness, strong passions, jealousy, sarcasm, with a selfish love of ease and comfort. He should cultivate selfcontrol, patience and an interest in the higher things of life.

Should build up self-esteem and work in those lines where he can express his social nature, or gather and correlate information for others, where originality is not required.

3. GEMINI—May 22 to June 21. Symbol, the twins. First air sign, governing the arms and hands.

This influence has the qualities of both 1 and 2, making it changeable, imaginative, high-strung. It indicates a dual personality, genial, sympathetic, generous, yet at other times the exact opposite. Full of clever ideas, versatile, adaptable, with energy, wit and sarcasm. It combines the creative ability of 1 with the tact of 2 and transforms mental images into concrete realities. It gives a love of the beautiful in nature and art, with fluency of speech and a magnetic personality. In order to be happy there must be variety and perfect freedom of expression; too much routine dampens the enthusiasm and brings the adverse nature into play.

The 3 defects evidence themselves in a restless disposition, going to extremes. He has plenty of ideas but lacks the continuity to bring them into complete expression. His independence leads him to override conventionality, and his strong passions make him susceptible to the wiles of the opposite sex. He should associate with people of strength and poise, learn to make decisions quickly, cultivate will power and develop his higher self.

4. CANCER—June 22 to July 22. Symbol, the crab. First water sign, governing the breasts.

This influence gives strong lungs and good breathing power, with the 4 qualities of mechanical and constructive ability, business sagacity, determination, perseverance, economy and painstaking effort. The Cancer individual succeeds well in business and manufacturing lines or in intellectual pursuits. He can be ruled through kindness but resents compulsion.

His defects are self-limitation, criticism, too great economy, and an over-cautious nature. He reasons himself out of his good intentions. It is very important for him to gain a good education if he does not always wish to be in a subservient position. He should associate with those of broad views and large interests.

5.   LEO---July 23 to August 23. Symbol, the lion. Second fire sign, governing the heart.

This influence gives a strong emotional love nature, with the charming, impulsive, fearless characteristics of the 5 vibration. The Leo individual is a splendid entertainer, full of youth and exuberant spirits, versatile, adaptable, with a pleasing and magnetic personality; very fond of the opposite sex. He must have personal freedom at all cost, the keynote of 5. Although he acts almost solely upon his intuition and is somewhat hasty in judgment, he is better fitted to rule than be ruled.

His defects, found in a 5, are aversion to study, quick anger, a selfish disregard for others, being ruled by his passions. He should develop will power and learn to take responsibilities, which will bring out his latent powers and give him the authority which he craves.

6.   VIRGO—August 24 to September 23. Symbol, the virgin. Second earth sign, governing the digestive organs.

This influence gives the strong mother, home-loving nature of the 6 vibration, with great talent in educational and literary lines. While it is materialistic in some respects and rather exclusive, when the spiritual nature is once developed the individual becomes a leader in all things which make for better homes, health and education. He is a protector of the rights of others rather than an originator or promoter, and succeeds well in either business or professional lines, especially as a writer, teacher or lecturer.

His faults are those of a reverse or negative 6—he talks too much and either refuses to assume responsibility or tries to take the burden of the world upon his shoulders. He should direct his attention to matters of health and education, and get into some position which requires expression on his part, when he will not have such a keen desire to criticize the efforts of others.

7.   LIBRA—September 24 to October 23. Symbol, the balance. Second air sign, governing the reins, the kidneys and reproductive system.

This influence gives strong intuition, with a love of refinement, beauty, luxury, and a desire for knowledge along many lines. The 7 attributes are strongly marked in the sensitive, persistent, positive nature, which finishes in a careful manner whatever one undertakes. Being guided by his intuitive faculties, this individual is gifted with remark-able foresight and reacts quickly to atmosphere and environment. He is fond of scientific and philosophical subjects, psychology, metaphysics and the mysteries of the occult, and could excel as a linguist, musician, writer or lecturer, or in any line requiring continuity of thought, discrimination, precision, and an inspirational insight into the nature of people or things.

The 7 defects which appear in this sign are egotism, pride and too great susceptibility to flattery and praise. It is hard for him to express what he feels. He should study public speaking, art, literature, character analysis, or anything which will develop his powers of self-expression. He should also take regular periods for rest and relaxation away from crowds and excitement.

8.   SCORPIO—October 24 to November 22. Symbol, the scorpion. Second water sign, governing the groin or sexual organs.

This influence gives to the individual the courage, confidence, dignity, keen discrimination, executive ability and energetic nature of the 8 vibration. Good judgment, practicality, diplomacy, tact, tenacity, together with a strong personality, make him an excellent judge, critic, politician, executive, public speaker or writer, wielding power with tongue or pen.

Adverse characteristics are criticism, intolerance, procrastination and an inclination to domineer and rule by fear. He allows suspicion and jealousy to blunt his powers. Should overcome any inferiority complex (another name for jealousy) and know that he will attract his own when he is that thing himself.

9.   SAGITTARIUS—November 23 to December 22. Symbol, the archer. Third fire sign, governing the thighs.

This influence gives the individual a sympathetic, whole-souled love (9) nature with energy, enthusiasm, and a genial, happy, jovial disposition. He likes everything on a large scale, and the first thing he is apt to do, when he falls heir to a legacy, is to tour the world, entertain his friends, give to his pet philanthropies, and then, if he has any money left, start a bank account. He has good chances for success as a musician, lawyer, actor, physician, preacher or teacher.

Some of his adverse characteristics are "nerves," quick temper, and the inability to make allowances for others. Should be careful to marry on his own intellectual and spiritual plane. Should learn to relax and conserve his energies.

10.   CAPRICORN—December 23 to January 20. Symbol, the goat. Third earth sign, governing the knees.

This influence gives the individual an independent, executive, forceful bearing, a high moral nature, ingenuity, and the organizing ability which naturally falls within the 10 vibration. He is a good manager, positive in his opinions, courageous in surmounting obstacles, public-spirited, self-confident, and makes an excellent teacher, writer or leader in any field, always keeping one foot firmly on the earth, no matter how high his aspirations climb.

Adverse characteristics are self-conceit, self-conscious-ness, egotism and a domineering attitude. He should have a thorough, all-round education and should associate with broad-minded and tolerant people.

11.   AQUARIUS—January 21 to February 19. Symbol, the water-bearer. Third air - governing the limbs.

This influence gives the individual a highly-strung nervous system, keen intuition, good judgment, and a pleasing hypnotic eye. He is an excellent judge of human nature, a good politician, convincing speaker, blessed with a saving sense of humor. He is ambitious for knowledge and eminently fitted to pass it on through writing, lecturing or other public avenues. He should direct his large imagination toward one end until that goal is achieved. He cares nothing for precedent; he is an 11 all over—always interested in making a new beginning, doing everything in a different way than it was ever done before.

Adverse characteristics are procrastination, prevarication, indolence, always seeking advice but accepting none; is apt to have an exaggerated ego. Should study metaphysics, psychology, character analysis and the occult sciences. Should cultivate punctuality and self-reliance and learn to be a good listener.

12.   PISCES—February 20 to March 21. Symbol, the fishes. Third water sign, governing the feet and ankles.

12 is the number of numerical completion. Its digits total 3, complete individual self-expression, with all the positive characteristics of the 1 and 2. The Pisces individual is an apt illustration of the 3 vibration, showing skill in art, with splendid opportunities for success in scientific, inventive and literary fields. He is magnetic, attractive, with an inspiring and helpful nature, a good observer, generous, sincere, sympathetic, but one who tends strictly to his own affairs. He is a great seeker after knowledge,

desiring to know the reason why in every situation. His adverse characteristics are lack of self-esteem, worrying about things which never happen and carrying a "chip" on his shoulder. He should learn to rely on his inner self, should maintain a cheerful attitude and choose a vocation which calls for creative self-expression.

The Cusps

Those born in the cusps partake of the characteristics of both signs. "Cusps," in astrology, are the beginning or first entrance of any "house" in the determination of nativities.

1. Aries and Taurus (1 and 2)—April 19-25.
2. Taurus and Gemini (2 and 3)—May 20-26.
3. Gemini and Cancer (3 and 4)—June 21-27.
4. Cancer and Leo (4 and 5)—July 22-28.
5. Leo and Virgo (5 and 6)—August 23-28.
6. Virgo and Libra (6 and 7)—September 23-29.
7. Libra and Scorpio (7 and 8)—October 23-29.
8. Scorpio and Sagittarius (8 and 9) November 22-28.
9. Sagittarius and Capricorn (9 and 10)—December 21-27.
10. Capricorn and Aquarius (10 and 11)—January 20-26.
11. Aquarius and Pisces (11 and 12)—February 19-25.
12. Pisces and Aries (12 and 1) March 21-27.

CHAPTER XVI

NUMBERS TELL THE TRUTH Illustrious Examples

THE most convincing proof of the truth of numbers is found by a visit to the halls of fame. A few examples will serve to show the accurate correspondence between the individual's life achievement and the dominant vibrations in his name.

Abraham Lincoln (1)

"LET us have faith that right makes might; and in that faith let us to the end dare to do our duty as we understand it."

```
                                                        Usual Signature
                    3        +      6     = 9   1   +    6        =7
Vowels:           1   1  1         9  6          1      9   6
                  ABRAHAM     LINCOLN          A.    LINCOLN
Consonants:   2 9   8   4    3  5 3  3 5            3   5 3  3 5
                    23              19                    19
                    5        +      11    = 6            10   =   10
Total name:        8        +       7  =15= 6    1  +    7     =   8
                         Born February 12, 1809
                                          18
                              2 + 3 + 9=14= 5 —Birth path.
```

Abraham Lincoln is the personification of the courageous, fearless "do and dare" spirit of the 3 "A"s of his first name and the 10 personality of Lincoln. A born leader, with the indomitable persistence of the true pioneer, his strong and striking individuality mingled with the crowd yet always remained as one apart. With a big heart (9) and a sensitive soul (7) he was able to get the viewpoint (1) of those about him, yet when it came to a crucial situation he discarded their advice and relied upon his God and his own intuition—the only path for a true 1 to follow if he desires success.

The 8 of Abraham and of "A. Lincoln" both show his large executive driving force, coupled with keen discrimination, tact and judgment. The 6 personality reveals his great interest in education and his conscientious sense of duty toward home and country. The vowel trinity of 3-6-9 not only gave him talent for law, but also the power to express his ideas with beauty and strength, in a clear, convincing manner.

His birth path of 5 shows that he came to work with humanity, to espouse the cause of freedom, to exercise power, and that in the legal profession (3 or 9) he would be most apt to find that outlet for free expression which his soul desired and which should eventually lead to his life work.

That he learned his lesson well and splendidly fulfilled his destiny6, the fearless assumption of large responsibilities—none doubt. His soul has gone on, yet whenever his name is mentioned the principles for which he stood are again broadcast to the universe by our own thought vibrations. Thus does his powerful influence still remain, through his name, to follow him forever.

The 2 Vibration

THE different editions of "Who's Who in America" are replete with Hannas who have been prominent in that special field of the 2 vibration, diplomacy. One of the most famous was the late Senator Marcus Alonzo (Mark) Hanna, who played such an important part in the political history of the United States during the days of President McKinley.

More recent figures of note are:

Hugh Henry Hanna, publicist, active in currency reform legislation, appointed by President Roosevelt in 1903 as chairman of the Commission on International Exchange.

$$
\begin{array}{cccccc}
 & & 2 & & -2 \\
\hline
 & 1 & & 1 & \\
H & A & N & N & A \\
8 & & 5 & 5 & \\
\hline
 & & 18 & & -9 \\
8 & 1 & 5 & 5 & 1 \\
\hline
 & & 23 & & -2 \\
\end{array}
$$

Hugh Sisson Hanna, economist, whose 2 talent for statistics brought him into public recognition through his services with the United States Bureau of Labor Statistics, 1908-1918, and gained for him the position of Chief Examiner of the National War Labor

Board in 1918-19. As an author his writings have dealt with accidents and their prevention, wages, labor laws and matters of finance.

Philip C. Hanna, recently retired Consul-General, active in foreign service, influential in preserving friendly relations with Mexico during the revolution in that country in 1914, now a lecturer on Latin American and international subjects.

Matthew Elting Hanna, present member of the diplomatic service at Washington, representative of the United States at German imperial maneuvers in 1911, with the American Embassy at Mexico from 1917 to 1921, since which time he has been in charge of Mexican affairs in the Department of State.

Ring W. Lardner (3): A WONDERFUL exponent of the humor of 3 is found in Ring W. Lardner, one of the most popular comedians (3) of all time.

$$
\begin{array}{lllll}
 & 9 & + & 6 & = 15 = (6) \\
\text{Vowels:} & 9 & & 1 \quad 5 & \textit{Without the "W"} \\
 & \text{R I N G} & \text{W.} & \text{L A R D N E R} & \text{Vowels — 6} \\
\text{Consonants:} & 9 \quad 5\,7 & 5 & 3 \quad 9\,4\,5 \quad 9 & \text{Cons. — 6} \\
 & 21 & & 30 & \text{Total — 3} \\
 & 3 + 5 & + & 3 & = (11) \\
\text{Total name:} & 9\,9\,5\,7 & 5 & 3\,1\,9\,4\,5\,5\,9 & \\
 & 30 & & 36 & \\
 & 3 + 5 & + & 9 & = 17 = (8) \\
 & \text{Born} & \text{March} & 6, \quad 1885 & \\
 & & 3 & + 6 + 22 & = (9\text{-}22)\text{—Birth path}
\end{array}
$$

With the total digit of 3 appearing four times in his name and again in his birth, how can this gentleman help being funny?

The complete trinity of literary expression, 3-6-9, is also found in both name and birth path, the latter total of 9-22 showing that he has come to be an outstanding figure in his line, bringing home to his readers, through his humor and imagination, the practical side of life in mirth-coated pills.

The 11 personality shows a winning vibration when it comes to making a striking, likable, dynamic impression upon other people. Even if we leave out the "W," which is frequently done, we still have a total of 6—one who can give splendid advice to the other fellow. This signature makes the vowels and consonants even, giving him absolute poise, with a good balance of sense and nonsense in the expression (3) of his art (3).

If anyone ever found his "right pew" it would seem that Mr. Lardner has, yet we would say that he has still larger worlds to conquer. His birth path of 9-22 shows that he has come, not only to cheer the world upon its way, but to remain active part in national affairs and in diplomatic circles.

Mary Pickford (4): MARY PICKFORD, one of the most loved film stars, is a splendid example of the wonderful achievement which can be made with the substantial 4 vibration.

```
                    8       +       6      =14= (5)
                                   ‾‾‾
                                   15
Vowels:          1   7           9       6
              M A R Y       P I C K F O R D
Consonants:   4     9       7   3 2 6   9 4
                 ‾‾‾‾‾           ‾‾‾‾
                  13              31
                   4       +       4          = (8)
Total name:   4 1 9 7       7 9 3 2 6 6 9 4
                ‾‾‾‾             ‾‾‾‾
                 21              46
                  3       +      10           =(4)

                Born April 8, 1893
                               ‾‾‾
                                21
                    4 + 8 +  3 =15=(6)—Birth path.
```

The general interpretation of number 4 is hard work and limitation, but when composed of 3 and 1, the positive, creative 1 accentuates the 3 powers of artistic ex-pression and makes the individual a keen intellectual builder (4) along lines of art (3) in no uncertain measure.

The 8 consonants show a strong personality, radiating an atmosphere of health, success and prosperity. The 5 vowels give an intense love of life from every angle with the ability to inject spice into all her activities. The 10 of Pickford not only bestows leadership qualities, but also a distinctive individuality, making her unique in her field.

She has been a most efficient (4) joy-bringer (3), putting the originality of 1 and the youth of 5 into the artistic expression (3) of those things which make the multitude happy. Her executive ability, good judgment and sense of values, evidenced by the two 8s and three 4s in her name, account for her success in business.

The lesson of her 6 birth path,—happy expression in service for others,—made up of 4-8-3, shows that the artistic talent of 3 and 6 will naturally fall in the field of imitation (4 and 8)—dramatic art.

It is significant to note that Mary Pickford made her reputation on the screen during the period of her life con-trolled by the 4 of her month (1-27) and that the name she chose carried the same vibration.

Jackie Coogan, the most famous boy star of the day, is also a 4, made up of 3 and 1. So, you who have the 4 vibration, cheer up! You may have to work, but if you are happy in doing it, and successful in bringing joy to others, you will likewise arrive—either at Hollywood or someplace better.

Woodrow Wilson (5 and 11): MANY are the Presidents of the United States who have predominated in the 5 vibration, answering the desire of the "United States" shown in its 5 vowels. A recent figure in the cause of universal freedom and lasting peace was the late Woodrow Wilson.

$$
\begin{array}{c}
\overline{9} \quad + \quad \overline{6} \quad =15=(6) \\
\textbf{Vowels:} \quad \overline{6\ 6} \quad 6 \quad \overline{9} \quad 6 \\
\textbf{W O O D R O W} \quad \textbf{W I L S O N} \\
\textbf{Consonants: 5} \quad 4\ 9 \quad 5 \quad 5\ 3\ 1 \quad 5 \\
\overline{5} \quad + \quad \overline{5} \quad =10=(1) \\
\textbf{Total:} \quad 5\ 6\ 6\ 4\ 9\ 6\ 5 \quad 5\ 9\ 3\ 1\ 6\ 5 \\
\overline{41} \quad \overline{29} \\
\overline{5} \quad + \quad \overline{11} \quad = (5\text{-}11) \\
\textbf{Born December 28, 1856} \\
12 \quad 10 \quad 20 \\
\overline{3} + \overline{1} + \overline{2} = (6)\text{—Birth date.} \\
\textbf{Higher aspect of path—}12 \quad 10 \\
\overline{22} \quad + \quad 2 = (22\text{-}2)
\end{array}
$$

5 appears four times in the above digit totals and in addition thereto is the first letter of both names, casting its broad humanitarian influence over the educational "0"s and total 6 vowels.

President Wilson's original name, Thomas Woodrow Wilson, with its 22 vowels and total of 22-5-11, certainly proclaimed a master soul whose destiny it was to project his high ideals into the heart of the universe.

As a historian (50), his writings are colored by the freedom and humanity aspect of the 5 vibration—"George 'Washin2-ton," "A History of the American People," "Free Life," "The New Freedom," "When a Man Con to Himself," "On Being Human," and many others of like character.

With a 6 birth vibration, as a college professor he was in his right vocation, which, when successfully mastered, led him into his larger destiny, teaching the higher truths to all mankind. Right here, however, we desire to call attention to the higher aspect of his birth path, revealed by the double numbers. December is the 12th month. Adding the month to the 10 day before reducing, we have

22, which with the 2 year makes his total vibration 22-2. Both 22 and 2 are diplomats and peacemakers, students of the laws of cause and effect, linking the spiritual with the material and striving to strike an even balance. As a university professor President Wilson was a splendid 6, but as a world leader (22) in the promotion of peace (2) he reached the heights of his higher calling.

Although he did not live to see realized the humanitarian principles for which he strove so mightily, his efforts were not lost. The strong positive thought currents of peace which he injected into the atmosphere have been gathering momentum ever since.

Theodore Roosevelt (22 and 5): ONE of the most powerful men of recent years, as well as one of the most popular, was Theodore Roosevelt, a typical 5, dominated by the 22 vibration.

```
                    22        +          22          =(22-22)
Vowels:           5 6   6    5        6 6   5   5
              T H E O D O R E    R O O S E V E L T
Consonants: 2 8      4    9        9   1   4   3 2
                    5          +         10              =(6)
Total:      2 8 5  64 6 9 5    9 6 6 1 5  4 5 3 2
                   45                    41
                    9          +          5         =14=(5)
          Born  October  27,  1858
                  10  +  9  =  22        =(10-22)—Birth path.
```

A born leader, diplomat and executive, Theodore Roosevelt brought his large 22 ideas into practical use for the benefit of the many., His fearlessness (1) and great personal magnetism, evidenced by the many 5s, gave him a wonderful influence over others, which his natural tact and diplomacy turned into constructive channels.

A lover of life from every angle, happy in world travel, he ran true to form even in sport as the greatest (22) hunter (5) of his day.

His contributions to American literature reveal the fluency of speech and the big heart of his 9 vibration, while the 6 personality shows his strong love for home and family.

Well did he learn his lesson of 1-22 and become an outstanding (1) figure in world affairs (22), a diplomat among diplomats, popular among foreign kings and queens as well as in his own country.

Jane Addams (6): THE pioneer home-maker among the women of the world is Jane Addams, founder of Hull House, in the city of Chicago.

```
                 6      +    2                        =(8)
Vowels:        1     5    1          1
             J A N E   A D D A M S
Consonants:  1     5    4 4     4 1
                 6      +         4            =(10)
Total:       1 1 5 5   1 4 4 1 4 1
                 ‾‾‾‾          ‾‾‾‾
                  12            15
                  ‾‾            ‾‾
                   3     +       6            =(9)
             Born September  6,  1860
                                 ‾‾‾
                                  15
              9  +  6  +  6  =21=(3)
```

The 6 vibration, of home, education and happy service to others, appears three times in the digits of the above name and twice in the birth path, while the strong positive force of the five is gives added power and authority to this illustrious woman who has established a world model community center where home-building is taught from every angle.

The complete trinity of balanced expression on the high plane is shown in her total digits of 8-9-10, the 8 giving her executive ability, diplomacy, tact, driving qualities; the 10, originality and the strength to stand her own ground despite public opinion or adverse circumstances; the 9, the ability to express her ideas in a large humanitarian way, with sympathy and understanding. The full name also contains the trinity of artistic and literary expression, 36-

9, enabling her to combine the esthetic side of life with the practicality of her many 4s.

As a peace envoy, visiting the governments of the world in the interest of peace, she represented the mothers of all time in their united prayer that wars shall cease.

Calvin Coolidge (7)—Henry Ford (7): TWO noteworthy individuals whose total names are both 7-7=14=5 and whose birthdays fall in the 7th month.

$$\frac{1\emptyset}{1\quad9} + \frac{8}{6\;6\quad9\quad\quad5} = (9) \qquad \frac{3}{5\quad\quad7} + \frac{6}{6} = (9)$$

$$\text{C A L V I N} \quad \text{C O O L I D G E} \qquad \text{H E N R Y} \quad \text{F O R D}$$

$$\frac{3\quad3\,4\quad5\quad3\quad\quad3\quad4\,7}{6} + \frac{8}{8} = 14 = (5) \qquad \frac{8\quad5\,9}{22} \qquad \frac{6\quad9\,4}{1\emptyset} = (22\text{-}1)$$

$$\frac{3\,1\,3\,4\,9\,5\quad3\,6\,6\,3\,9\,4\,7\,5}{\frac{25}{7}} + \frac{43}{7} = 14 = (5) \qquad \frac{8\,5\,5\,9\,7}{\frac{34}{7}} + \frac{6\,9\,9\,4}{\frac{15}{7}} = 4 = (5)$$

Born July 4, 1872   Born July 30, 1843

$$\frac{7\quad4\quad\quad18}{11} + \frac{18}{9} = (11\text{-}9) \qquad\qquad \frac{13}{7 + 3 + 9} = 19 = (1\emptyset)$$

In Chapter IX particular reference is made to the important events which have occurred in President Coolidge's life in yearly cycles of 7.

Both of these men, supreme in their realm, typify the strength, firmness, solidarity and large achievement of the true 7 vibration. They rely on their own intuition and keep well their own counsel, directing the activities of others with confidence and poise.

5 is usually considered a charitable number, but the unusual power which rests in the hands of these two men is due to the stabilizing force of the two 7s, which brings continuity of thought, will power, perfection of detail and thoroughness of execution into every

project. 5 always denotes an investigative mind and brims many interesting experiences to pass in the life of the individual, but when made up of 7 plus 7 it is a vibration of unusual accomplishment, combining intuition with wisdom and an instinctive understanding of human nature with the power to rule.

Another illustrious example is found in George Washington, whose destiny (full name) was 7 and whose vowels had the magic vibration of 7-7 = 14=5.

Maude Adams (8)—Colonel Goethals (8): THE two widely divergent aspects of the 8 vibration are aptly shown in the celebrated actress of Peter Pan fame and the noted engineer who brought to completion the great Panama Canal.

$$\frac{0}{1\ 3\ \overline{5}} + \frac{2}{1\ \overline{1}} = (11)$$

M A U D E   A D A M S

$$\frac{4}{} \quad \frac{4}{} \qquad \frac{4}{} \quad \frac{4}{}\ 1$$

$$\overline{8} \qquad + \qquad \overline{9} \qquad = 17 = (8)$$

$$4\ 1\ 3\ 4\ 5 \qquad 1\ 4\ 1\ 4\ 1$$

$$\frac{17}{} \qquad\qquad \frac{11}{}$$

$$\overline{8} \qquad + \qquad \overline{11} \qquad = (8\text{-}11)$$

Born November 1', 1872

$$\overline{18}$$

$$11 \qquad 11 \qquad 9 = (11\text{-}11\text{-}9)$$

$$\frac{7}{5\ 6\ \overline{5}} + \frac{7}{1\ 9\ \text{u}} + \frac{3}{6\ 5\ \overline{1}} \qquad = 17 = (8)$$

GEORGE   WASHINGTON   GOETHALS

$$\frac{8}{6\ 0\ \overline{5}} + \frac{3}{6\ 5\ \overline{1}} \qquad = (11)$$

C O L O N E L   G O E T H A L S

$$\frac{3}{}\ 3\ 5\ 3 \qquad 7\ 2\ 8\ 3\ 1$$

$$\overline{5} \qquad + \qquad \overline{3} \qquad = (8)$$

$$3\ 6\ 3\ 6\ 5\ 5\ 3 \qquad 7\ 6\ 5\ 2\ 8\ 1\ 3\ 1$$

$$\frac{31}{} \qquad\qquad \frac{3\ }{}$$

$$\overline{4} \qquad + \qquad \text{0} \qquad = (10)$$

Born June 2?, 1858

$$6 \qquad 11 \qquad = (6\text{-}11\text{-}22)$$

Maude Adams certainly has all the vibrations which could be desired to attract unusual renown. Her vowels give natural inspiration (11) in the line of dramatic (2) art (9) while her birth path of 11-11-9 shows that she has come to gain universal (1 1) fame in her chosen vocation.

The mere sound of her name creates the impression that here is an individual with a strong 8 personality, executive ability and tact,, who radiates the prosperity atmosphere, while the total 8 of Maude and in her full signature gives marked success, not only in the field of imitation, but also in business and financial avenues as well.

Wisely did she choose when she took this powerful nom de plume through which to gain outstanding (11) success in dramatic (8) art (9).

Colonel Goethals' talent in engineering (8) is found in the vowels of his original name, while the two 7s help to make his work a model of perfection and completion. The name whose vibration he has carried for many years reveals a strong executive, forceful 8 personality, while his 11-vowel total throws its leadership qualities over the 8 of Colonel, giving him driving force and unusual engineering ability. This he also turned to good account in solving the large health (3) problems which confronted him at every turn in the Canal Zone.

His high birth vibrations show that he came to render a humanitarian service (6) of universal magnitude (11 and 22). 22 is a diplomatic executive, one who brings peace and harmony between opposing factions. In building (8) the Panama Canal Colonel Goethals joined two great oceans, resulting in an increase of business, commerce and, friendly relations between all peoples.

Irvin S. Cobb (9): IRVIN S. COBB, whose first name shows the 9 vibration in three aspects, is a wonderful example of the 9 literary genius who travels the globe in search of new adventures with which to punctuate his fluent expression.

$$9 \qquad + \qquad 6 \qquad =15=(6)$$

$$\overline{9} \quad \overline{9} \qquad\qquad \overline{6}$$

I R V I N   S.   C O B B
   9 4   5   1   3   2 2

$$\overline{9} \quad + \quad \overline{1} \quad + \quad \overline{7} \quad =17=(8)$$

9 9 4 9 5   1   3 6 2 2

$$\overline{36} \qquad\qquad \overline{13}$$

$$\overline{9} \quad + \quad 1 \quad + \quad \overline{4} \quad =14=(5)$$

Born June 23, 1876
   6   5   22

$$\overline{11} \qquad\qquad =(11\text{-}22)\text{—Birth path.}$$

A genial, whole-souled fellow, with large humanitarian ideas, interested in world affairs, is this noted American humorist. Every vibration is present in his name, showing his ability to contact the minds of all classes.

9 being 3 X3, gives him abundant humor and sympathetic understanding of human nature, while the 5 makes him an eternal investigator, putting the exuberance of youth into all of his activities. The 1 of "S" adds strength and originality to his splendid building (4) power in the artistic (9) handling of words.

His birth path shows that he has come to render a large (11-22) joy-bringing service (6) to humanity (5) and that especially between the ages of 27 and 54 will his life be filled with varied experiences and much travel (5). His reputation has already encircled the globe, yet we venture to say that after 54, when he comes into the 22 vibration of his year, he will take a more prominent part in world affairs than ever before. Then will he speak, not only with a mirthprovoking humor, but with the power, force and far-reaching influence of a true diplomat.

Napoleon Bonaparte (11)—David Wark Griffith (11): ONE of the most dynamic characters of all history was Napoleon Bonaparte.

Though short of stature, he moved the world and is a splendid illustration of the conquering power which lies within every 11 vibration.

```
          9              +                     4              =13=(4)
    1    6    5   6            6    1    1        5
    N  A  P  L  E  O  N      B  O  N  A  P  A  R  T  E
    5    7    3       5      2    5    7       9  2
             20             +               7              =(9)
    5  1  7  6  3  5  6  5   2  6  5  1  7  1  9  2  5
             38                            38
             11             +              11             =(11-11)
         Born  August  15,  1808
                             17
          8  +  6  +  8 =(22)---Birth path.
```

Napoleon's birth path, with its two 8s and master 22, shows that as a general and engineer of military affairs he was in his true calling. With his strong executive, driving force (8), his keen intellect (4) and unusual inspiration (11-11), he used his strong personality (9) to promote (1 1) his great ambitions and become the conqueror of the then known world.

His fall came through the reversal of his own strong forces upon him, caused by his greed for personal fame and glory. An 11 is a dynamic force with far-reaching influence, but the minute the individual ceases to use his power for the universal good and tries to bend the world for his own selfish interests, that minute he invites his own destruction.

In his forward move for accomplishment, Napoleon swept the continent, but when he failed to give back to the world its due, the reflex current of his own vibrations returned with disaster in its path and sent him to St. Helena. Such is the finish of all 1 is and 22s who do not work unselfishly for the good of all. It is impossible to confine 11 pounds of pressure in the individual boiler built only for 7 without causing an explosion.

"Freely ye have received, freely give," should be em-blazoned upon the mirrors of all 1 1s and 22s. Life with them is expansion or extinction.

A modern 11 in a different field is David `'Nark Griffith (name set out in Chapter III), who, with an 11 soul, a dynamic 1-11 personality and the large destiny of 22-8-11, has conquered the world in his own particular realm.

Ruth J. Maurer (22 and 9): RUTH J. MAURER, founder and head of Marinello, the largest teaching organization of beauty culture in the world, with schools in all the principal cities of the United States, is one of the most outstanding business women of the present day. She is a • splendid example of the large success which attends the 22 who uses his business acumen, tact and organizing qualities in the promotion of a big, practical, humanitarian idea, beneficial to many instead of a few.

Note the four positions of 22 in this name, the double aspect of 11,—in personality and key-note,—and the manner in which the 9 vibration permeates the whole—as the first letter of entire name, as vowel total of surname, and by its more frequent occurrence than any other digit.

```
  3             +        9      =12=(3)—Soul—
                     1  3   5              subconscious desire.
R U T H   J.   M  A  U  R  E  R
9   2 8   1    4        9     9
      10        1          22          =(11-22)— Personality.
9 3 2 8   1    4  1  3  9  5  9
                       31
  22           1        4          =(22-5)—Present plane
                                         of action.
```

	1 — 2 — 3	4 — 5 — 6 — 7	8 —9
Number of time each letter occurs in name:	2 1 2	1 1 — —	1 3

11 letters — Key-note (11)

With the most powerful personality that anyone could have (11-22) Mrs. Maurer threw her leadership qualities in the line of her predominating digit, 9,—"sympathy and understanding, with inspiration and artistic expression on a world scale," and brought to bear upon this complete triangle of success, 9-1 1-22, her birth path digit of 6,—"humanitarian service in the realm of beauty, home, health and education."

The 22 in the given name proclaims a master intellect, with organizing and business talent. That she really used this force constructively and thereby attracted still greater power, is shown by its second appearance in the consonants of her married name, adding to her natural wisdom in-creased executive ability with which to carry out her comprehensive educational program.

As a 22-5 Mrs. Maurer is not only the builder (22) of a world-wide sales (5) organization, but a master (22) psychologist (5) as well, blessed with a keen understanding of human nature. In the development of her own original (1) idea she chose a high name vibration in keeping with her special line (Marinello totals 9) and established (4) a unique and outstanding (1) system of beauty (3 and 9) instruction (6), famed throughout the world (9).

With a 22 breadth of view which led her to investigate (5) all lines of thought and endeavor she has used the vibratory laws of Numerology, Psychology, Astrology, as well as the "so-called" more practical sciences, to attract success from the universe, taking pains to observe the best time and place for dealing with any important subject and to properly name any new product before placing it upon the market.

As a writer Mrs. Maurer has also expressed her vocational 6 (total digit of her birth date) in a masterful 22 way, bringing her inspirational ideas down to earth in a practical and interesting manner, sending out new life (5) vibrations to all who read her pages. Through helping others to a better understanding she has reaped a reward far beyond her expectations, and although the attendant wealth and fame have placed her in the fore-most rank, her interests are still paramount in the pro-motion of constructive thought and new lines of human betterment.

Living up to the demands of her own vibrations, Mrs. Maurer has attracted "her own" in a like universal manner. Thus should every 22 aim to pour his forces through the avenue of his strongest vibrations, in the direction indicated by his birth path, working with a big idea for the benefit of many, if he desires a rich blessing to follow.

CONCLUSION

MAY health, harmony and success, in large measure, attend the ambitious soul who has read thus far. To aid you in working out your individual problem, we have appended a list of over 1,500 names with their vowel, consonant and total number values. Remember, however, that, whatever your lesson or name may be, there is power in every number when you conform in truth to its higher nature and attune your life to its dominant note.

May your knowledge of the law prosper you and each day be filled with vibrations of peace, happiness and glorious achievement.

Let naught deter you from your goal,

But be the master of your soul,

Knowing well the spoken word

From the vibrant ether of your world

Creates the form you hold in mind.

Think not your aim can be too high:

DESIRE the goal cloth prophesy,

And nothing is impossible; For the

Law, which stands invincible,

Returns to you your thoughts in kind.

APPENDIX:

1,500 Names and Their Number Values

The first number after each name shows its total value; the second number its vowel total, and the third, its consonant total.

Aaron - - - 22—8-5	Adam - - - 10—2-8
Abbe - - - 10—6-4	Adams - - - 11—2-9
Abbie - - - 10—6-4	Addison - - - 3—7-5
Abbot - - - 4—7-6	Adel - - - - 4—6-7
Abel - - - 11—6-5	Adela - - - - 5—7-7
Aberdeen - - - 9—7-2	Adelaide - - 5—3-11
Abigail - - - 5—2-3	Adelon - - - 6—3-3
Abihu - - - 5—4-10	Adelphi - - 10—6-22
Abijah - - 22—11-11	Adler - - - 22—6-7
Abilene - - - 3—2-10	Adonais - - - 9—8-10
Abner - - - 22—6-7	Adonis - - - 8—7-10
Abraham - - - 8—3-5	Adrian - - 11—11-9
Abram - - - 8—2-6	Aeneas - - - 9—3-6
Abruzzo - - 10—10-9	Aeolia - - - 7—22-3
Absalom - - - 9—8-10	Aeschylus - - 5—7-7
Achates - - - 3—7-5	Aesop - - - 2—3-8
Achilles - - - 6—6-9	Agard - - - 22—2-2
Ackerman - - 3—7-5	Agatha - - - 2—3-8
Acla - - - 8—2-6	Agnes - - - 10—6-4
Aconcio - - 6—22-11	Agricola - - 3—8-22
Acres - - - 10—6-4	Agrippa - - - 5—11-3
Acton - - - 8—7-10	Ahab - - - - 3—2-1
Ada - - - - 6—2-4	Aida - - - - 6—11-4
Adair - - - 6—11-4	Aikin - - - - 8—1-7
Adalbert - - 9—7-2	Ainsworth - - 10—7-3
Adalia - - - 10—3-7	Aitken - - - 6—6-9
Adaline - - 10—7-3	Ajax - - - - 9—2-7

Alameda - - 10—8-11	Alta - - - - 7—2-5
Alamo - - - 6—8-7	Alton - - 8—7-10
Alba - - - - 7—2-5	Alva - - - - 9—2-7
Albert - - - 22—6-7	Alvarado - - 11—9-2
Alberta - - - 5—7-7	Alvarez - - - 4—7-6
Albina - - - 3—11-10	Amanda - - - 7—3-4
Albinus - - - 6—4-11	Amber - - - 3—6-6
Alcott - - - 8—7-10	Ambrose - - 10—3-7
Alcyone - - - 3—1-11	Amelia - - - 5—7-7
Aldan - - - 5—2-3	America - - - 5—7-7
Alden - - - 9—6-3	Ames - - - 11—6-5
Aldine - - - 9—6-3	Amie - - - 10—6-4
Aldred - - - 8—6-2	Amy - - - - 3—8-4
Aldrich - - 10—10-9	Anabel - - - 8—7-10
Alene - - - 10—11-8	Ananias - - - 5—3-11
Alesia - - - 2—7-4	Anastasia - - 22—4-9
Alexander - - 3—3-9	Andersen - - 8—11-6
Alexandra - - 8—8-9	Anderson - - - 9—3-6
Alexis - - - 7—6-10	Andre - - - 6—6-9
Alfaro - - - 8—8-9	Andrew - - - 11—6-5
Alfonso - - - 10—4-6	Andrews - - - 3—6-6
Alfred - - - 10—6-22	Angel - - - 3—6-6
Alice - - - - 3—6-6	Angelina - - - 9—7-2
Alicia - - - 8—2-6	Angelo - - - 9—3-6
Alise - - - - 10—6-4	Anita - - - 9—11-7
Alla - - - - 8—2-6	Ann - - - 11—1-10
Allan - - - 4—2-11	Anna - - - 3—2-10
Allen - - - 8—6-11	Annabelle - - 3—3-9
Allie - - - - 3—6-6	Anne - - - 7—6-10
Allison - - - 10—7-3	Annie - - - 7—6-10
Alma - - - - 9—2-7	Anson - - - 9—7-11
Alonzo - - - 11—4-7	Anthony - - - 7—5-2

105

Anton - - - 10—7-3	Aurelius - - - 7—3-4
Antonio - - - 7—22-3	Aurora - - 11—11-9
Aphrodite - - 6—3-3	Austin - - - 3—4-8
Apollo - - - 8—4-4	Ava - - - - 6—2-4
Apollos - - - 9—4-5	Avalon - - - 2—8-3
Aquila - - - 7—5-11	Avis - - - 6—10-5
Archer - - - 8—6-11	Avon - - - - 7—7-9
Archibald - - 4—11-11	Bab - - - - 5—1-4
Arden - - - 6—6-9	Babbitt - - 2—10-10
Ariel - - - - 9—6-3	Babcock - - - 10—7-3
Arion - - - 3—7-5	Bach - - - - 5—1-4
Arles - - - 10—6-4	Bacon - - - 8—7-10
Arlo - - - 10—7-3	Bain - - - 8—10-7
Arne - - - - 2—6-5	Baird - - - 7—10-6
Arno - - - - 3—7-5	Baker - - - 10—6-4
Arnold - - - 10—7-3	Balbo - - - - 5—7-7
Arthur - - - 5—4-10	Baldwin - - 11—10-10
Asa - - - - 3—2-1	Balfour - - - 3—10-2
Asher - - - - 6—6-9	Ball - - - - 9—1-8
Ashland - - - 5—2-3	Ballou - - - 9—10-8
Ashton - - - 5—7-7	Balzac - - - 9—2-7
Aster - - - - 9—6-3	Bana - - - - 9—2-7
Astor - - - 10—7-3	Bancroft - - - 7—7-9
Atchison - - 8—7-10	Banks - - - 11—1-10
Athalia - - - 7—3-4	Bara - - - - 4—2-11
Aubrey - - - 9—9-9	Barbara - - - 7—3-22
Auburn - - - 5—7-7	Barclay - - - 8—2-6
Audrey - - - 11—9-2	Bardell - - - 9—6-3
Auerbach - - 5—10-4	Barker - - - 10—6-22
Augusta - - 9—8-10	Barlow - - 8—7—10
Augustine - - 9—3-6	Barnabas - - 22—3-10
Aurelia - - 4—10-3	Barnaby - - - 9—9-9

106

Barnard - - - 4—2-11	Belinda - - - 11—6-5
Barnes - - - 5—6-8	Bell - - - - 4—5-8
Barnett - - - 8—6-2	Bella - - - - 5—6-8
Barnum - - - 6—4-2	Belle - - - 9—10-8
Barodel - - - 3—3-9	Ben - - - - 3—5-7
Baron - - - 5—7-7	Benedict - - 8—10-7
Barr - - - - 3—1-2	Benjamin - - 5—6-8
Barrett - - - 3—6-6	Bennett - - 8—10-7
Barrington - - 10—7-3	Benno - - - 5—11-3
Barron - - - 5—7-7	Benson - - - 6—11-4
Barry - - - 10—8-2	Berlin - - - 6—5-10
Bart - - - - 5—1-4	Bernard - - 8—6-11
Barthold - - 8—7-10	Berne - - - 8—10-7
Bartholomew - - 6—9-6	Bernhardt - - 9—6-3
Bartlett - - - 8—6-2	Berry - - - - 5—3-2
Barton - - - 7—7-9	Bert - - - - 9—5-4
Basil - - - 7—10-6	Bertha - - - 9—6-3
Bassett - - - 5—6-8	Bertini - - - 5—5-9
Bastian - - 3—11-10	Bertram - - - 5—6-8
Bates - - - 11—6-5	Bess - - - - 9—5-4
Bauer - - - 2—9-11	Besse - - - 5—10-4
Baxter - - - 7—6-10	Bethel - - - 7—10-6
Bayard - - - 6—2-22	Betty - - - - 9—3-6
Beall - - - - 5—6-8	Beulah - - - 22—9-4
Beatrice - - - 9—2-7	Beverly - - - 8—8-9
Beatrix - - - 7—6-10	Bianca - - - 3—11-10
Becker - - - 8—10-7	Biglow - - - 5—6-8
Becky - - - 10—3-7	Bill - - - - 8—9-8
Bede - - - 7—10-6	Billings - - - 3—9-3
Bedell - - 22—10-3	Birch - - - 4—9-22
Beecher - - - 10—6-22	Bird - - - - 6—9-6
Birdie - - - 11—5-6	Beethoven - - 6—3-3

Biron - - - - 4—6-7	Brisbane - - 7—6-10
Bismarck - - 4—10-3	Brock - - - 22—6-7
Black - - - 11—1-10	Brooks - - - 8—3-5
Blaine - - - 7—6-10	Bruce - - - 22—8-5
Blair - - - 6—10-5	Bruno - - - 7—9-7
Blake -- - - 4—6-7	Buchanan - - 10—5-5
Blanchard - - 9—2-7	Buck - - - 10—3-7
Blanche - - - 9—6-3	Bunyan - - 5—4-10
Blanco - - - 2—7-4	Burgess - - 10—8-2
Blane - - - 7—6-10	Burke - - - - 3—8-4
Boaz - - - 8—7-10	Burt - - - - 7—3-4
Bob - - - - 10—6-4	Burton - - - 9—9-9
Bobs - - - 11—6-5	Butler - - - 6—8-7
Bonaparte - - 11—4-7	Byron - - - 11—4-7
Bonheur - - - 11—5-6	Cadmus - - - 7—4-3
Bonne - - - 5—11-3	Cadwaller - - 7—7-9
Bonnie - - - 5—2-3	Caesar - - - 2—7-4
Booth - - - - 6—3-3	Cain - - - 9—10-8
Bowles - - 22—11-11	Calve - - - 7—6-10
Boyd - - - 10—4-6	Calvert - - - 9—6-3
Boyle - - - - 5—9-5	Calvin - - - 7—10-6
Bradford - - - 5—7-7	Cameron - - - 6—3-3
Bradshaw - - 4—2-11	Camilla - - - 6—11-4
Bradstreet - - 4—11-11	Campbell - - 10—6-22
Brady - - - - 5—8-6	Cannon - - - 7—7-9
Bragg - - - - 8—1-7	Captain - - 10—11-8
Brand - - - 3—1-2	Carl - - - 7—1-6
Brewster - - 11—10-10	Carlisle - - - 7—6-10
Brian - - - 8—10-7	Carlos - - - 5—7-7
Brice - - - 10—5-5	Carlyle - - - 4—4-9
Briggs - - - 8—9-8	Carmel - - 7—6-10
Bright - - 10—9-10	Carolina - - 10—8-2

Caroline - - -	5—3-2	Clarence - -	7—11-5
Carolyn - - -	7—5-2	Claribel - - -	8—6-2
Carrie - - - -	9—6-3	Clarice - - -	6—6-9
Carroll - - -	7—7-9	Clarinda - - -	8—11-6
Caruso - - -	5—10-4	Clarissa - -	10—11-8
Carver - - -	4—6-7	Clark - - -	9—1-8
Cary - - - -	2—8-3	Clarke - - -	5—6-8
Casimir - -	9—10-8	Claude - -	10—9-10
Catharine - - -	7—7-9	Claudia - -	6—5-10
Catherine - -	11—2-9	Clayton - - -	9—7-2
Cecil - - - -	5—5-9	Clemens - -	8—10-7
Cecilia - - -	6—6-9	Cleopatra - -	10—4-6
Celeste - - -	6—6-9	Cleveland - -	6—11-22
Celestine - -	11—6-5	Clifford - -	10—6-4
Charles - - -	3—6-6	Clinton - - -	6—6-9
Charlie - - -	11—6-5	Clio - - - -	3—6-6
Charlotte - - -	3—3-9	Clive - - -	6—5-10
Chester - - -	6—10-5	Clyde - - -	22—3-10
Chicago - - -	10—7-3	Clytie - - -	11—3-8
Chloe - - -	7—11-5	Cobb - - - -	4—6-7
Chopin - - -	11—6-5	Cole - - - -	8—11-6
Christian - -	11—10-10	Coleridge - - -	6—7-8
Christiana - -	3—2-10	Coles - - -	9—11-7
Christina - -	11—10-10	Collier - - -	11—2-9
Christine - -	6—5-10	Collins - - -	3—6-6
Christopher - -	4—2-11	Colonel - - -	4—8-5
Christy - - -	3—7-5	Colton - - -	7—3-4
Cicero - - -	8—2-6	Columbus - -	7—3-4
Cinderella - -	11—2-9	Conner - - -	6—11-22
Circe - - -	11—5-6	Conrad - - -	10—7-3
Clara - - - -	8—2-6	Constance - -	4—3-10
Clare - - - -	3—6-6	Conway - - -	9—7-2

Cook - - - - 8—3-5	Daniel - - - 9—6-3
Cooke - - - 22—8-5	Dante - - - 8—6-11
Cooper - - - 9—8-10	Daphne - - - 3—6-6
Cora - - - 10—7-3	Darby - - - - 5—8-6
Corinne - - - 6—2-22	Darcy - - - - 6—8-7
Cornelia - - - 5—3-2	Darius - - - 9—4-5
Cornelius - - - 8—5-3	Darling - - 11—10-10
Cornwall - - 7—7-10	Darwin - - - 6—10-5
Cozzens - - - 9—11-7	David - - - 22—10-3
Crane - - - - 5—6-8	Davies - - - 6—6-9
Crawford - - 7—7-9	Davis - - - 10—10-9
Cristobel - - - 4—2-2	Dean - - - - 6—6-9
Cromwell - - 11—11-9	Deborah - - - 8—3-5
Cullen - - - 22—8-5	Decker - - 10—10-9
Cummins - - 11—3-8	Dee - - - - 5—10-4
Curtis - - - - 9—3-6	Defoe - - - 8—7-10
Curtiss - - - 10—3-7	Delano - - - 6—3-3
Cushing - - - 9—3-6	Delia - - - 22—6-7
Culver - - - 9—8-10	Della - - - 7—6-10
Cynthia - - - 8—8-9	Delos - - - 10—11-8
Cyrene - - - 7—8-8	Delphi - - - 9—5-22
Cyril - - - - 4—7-6	Demosthenes - - 10—3-7
Cyrus - - - 5—10-4	Denis - - - 6—5-10
Dagmar - - - 8—2-6	Dennie - - - 6—10-5
Daisy - - - 22—8-5	Dennis - - - 11—5-6
Dalby - - - - 8—8-9	Depew - - - 8—10-7
Dale - - - - 4—6-7	Desmond - - 11—11-9
Dalton - - - 3—7-5	Dessa - - - - 3—6-6
Damon - - - 2—7-4	Dewitt - - - 9—5-4
Dan - - - 10—1-9	Dexter - - - 4—10-3
Dana - - - 11—2-9	Diana - - - 2—11-9
Danby - - - 10—8-11	Diaz - - - 22—10-3

Dick - - - - 9—9-9	Durham - - - 11—4-7
Dickson - - - 3—6-6	Dutch - - - - 2-—3-8
Dickens - - - 11—5-6	Dwight - - - 8—9-8
Disraeli - - - 5—6-8	Dyer - - - - 7—3-4
Dodge - - - 8—11-6	Earl - - - - 9—6-3
Dolly - - - 5—4-10	Earle - - - 5—11-3
Dolores - - - 7—8-8	Ed - - - - 9—5-4
Don - - - - 6—6-9	Eda - - - - 10—6-4
Donald - - - 5—7-7	Eddy - - - - 2—3-8
Dora - - - - 2—7-4	Edgar - - - - 8—6-2
Doris - - - 11—6-5	Edison - - - 3—2-10
Dorothea - - - 5—9-5	Edith - - - 10—5-5
Dorothy - - 6—10-5	Editha - - - 11—6-5
Dot - - - - 3—6-6	Edmund - - - 7—8-8
Douglas - - - 7—10-6	Edna - - - - 6—6-9
Doyle - - - - 7—9-7	Edsel - - - 9—10-8
Drake - - - - 3—6-6	Edward - - 10—6-22
Draper - - - 8—6-11	Edwin - - - 10—5-5
Drexel - - - 5—10-22	Edythe - - - 4—8-5
Drummond - - 3—9-3	Egan - - - - 9—6-3
Drusilla - - - 6—4-2	Elaine - - - 10—2-8
Dryden - - - 7—3-22	Elba - - - - 11—6-5
Duane - - - 9—9-9	Eldred - - - 3—10-2
Dudley - - - 8—8-9	Eleanor - - - 7—8-8
Duke - - - - 5—8-6	Eli - - - - 8—5-3
Dulce - - - 9—8-10	Elias - - - 10—6-4
Dumas - - - 4—4-9	Elihu - - - 10—8-11
Duncan - - - 3—4-8	Elijah - - - - 9—6-3
Dunkirk - - - 7—3-22	Elisha - - - - 9—6-3
Dupont - - - 9—9-9	Elissa - - - - 2—6-5
Dupre - - - 10—8-2	Eliza - - - 8—6-11
Durand - - - 8—4-22	Elizabeth - - - 7—2-5

Ella - - - - 3—6-6	Ethelyn - - - 8—8-9
Ellean - - 22—11-11	Eugene - - - 3—9-3
Elliott - - - 3—2-1	Eugenia - - - 8—5-3
Ellis - - - - 3—5-7	Evan - - - - 6—6-9
Ellsworth - - 6—11-4	Evans - - - 7—6-10
Elmer - - - 8—10-7	Eva - - - - 10—6-4
Elmira - - - 4—6-7	Eve - - - - 5—10-4
Eloise - - - 11—7-4	Evelyn - - - 11—8-3
Elsie - - - 5—10-4	Everett - - - 5—6-8
Elsworth - - 3—11-10	Ewing - - - 4—5-8
Elysia - - - 8—22-4	Ezra - - - - 5—6-8
Emanuel - - - 8—5-3	Fairbanks - - 9—11-7
Emerson - - 8—7-10	Fairchild - - 7—10-6
Emery - - - 3—8-4	Fairfax - - 11—11-9
Emilia - - - 4—6-7	Faith - - - 8—10-7
Emily - - - 10—3-7	Fan - - - - 3—1-11
Emma - - - 5—6-8	Fannie - - - 4—6-7
Emmet - - 2—10-10	Fanny - - - 6—8-7
Emmons - - 7—11-5	Farmer - - - 7—6-10
Emory - - - 4—9-4	Farnham - - - 7—2-5
Enid - - - - 5—5-9	Farrar - - - 8—2-6
Enos - - - - 8—11-6	Father - - - 4—6-7
Ephraim - - - 7—6-1	Fatima - - - 5—11-3
Erastus - - - 22—9-4	Faust - - - - 4—4-9
Eric - - - - 8—5-3	Fay - - - - 5—1-4
Erma - - - 10—6-4	Faye - - - 10—6-4
Ermine - - 10—10-9	Felice - - - 4—10-3
Ernest - - - 9—10-8	Felix - - - 11—5-6
Ernestine - - 10—6-22	Fenwick - - - 8—5-3
Estelle - - - 6—6-9	Ferdinand - - 3—6-6
Esther - - - 3—10-2	Ferguson - - 6—5-10
Ethel - - - 5—10-4	Fern - - - - 7—5-2

Fernandez - - 3—11-10	Freda - - - 7—6-10
Finlay - - - 4—10-3	Frederick - - 7—10-6
Fischer - - - 5—5-9	Fredericka - - 8—2-6
Fisher - - - 11—5-6	Fredrick - - 11—5-6
Fisk - - - - 9—9-9	Freeman - - 8—11-6
Fiske - - - - 5—5-9	Frieda - - - 7—6-10
Fitch - - - 10—9-10	Fritz - - - - 7—9-7
Fitzgerald - - 9—6-3	Fuller - - - 11—8-3
Flavia - - - 6—11-4	Fulton - - - 7—9-7
Fleming - - - 3—5-7	Gabriel - - - 9—6-3
Fletcher - - 5—10-4	Gaby - - - - 8—8-9
Flint - - - - 7—9-7	Gaines - - - 10—6-4
Flo - - - - 6—6-9	Gail - - - 2—10-10
Flora - - - - 7—7-9	Gale - - - - 7—6-10
Florence - - - 6—7-8	Galicia - - - 6—2-4
Florian - - - 3—7-5	Garcia - - - 3—11-10
Flower - - - 7—11-5	Garden - - - 4—6-7
Floyd - - - - 8—4-4	Garibaldi - - - 9—2-7
Forbes - - - 11—11-9	Garnet - - - 11—6-5
Ford - - - - 7—6-10	Garrick - - - 4—10-3
Forrest - - - 11—11-9	Gary - - - - 6—8-7
Fortuna - - 5—10-22	Gascon - - - 5—7-7
Fortune - - - 9—5-22	Gaston - - - 22—7-6
Foster - - - 11—11-9	Gates - - - - 7—6-10
Fowler - - - 7—11-5	Gayelord - - - 6—3-3
Fox - - - - 9—6-3	Gaylord - - - 10—7-3
Frances - - - 3—6-6	Gaze - - - - 3—6-6
Francis - - - 7—10-6	Gene - - - 22—10-3
Francisca - - 11—11-9	Geneva - - - 9—11-7
Frank - - - 5—1-22	Genevieve - - 4—11-2
Franklin - - - 4—10-3	George - - - 3—7-5
Fred - - - - 6—5-10	Georgia - - - 8—3-5

Georgiana - -	5—22-10	Graves - - - 9—6-3
Georgine - -	8—7-10	Gray - - - - 6—1-5
Gerald - - -	11—6-5	Grayling - - 3—10-11
Geraldine - -	3—2-1	Green - - - 4—10-3
Gerard - - -	8—6-11	Greene - - - 9—6-3
Gerry - - -	10—3-7	Gregory - - - 5—9-5
Gertrude - - -	8—4-4	Griffith - - 11—9-11
Gibbons - - -	5—6-8	Grimes - - - 8—5-3
Gibson - - -	3—6-6	Grimm - - - 6—9-6
Gideon - - -	9—2-7	Griselda - - - 3—6-6
Gilbert - - -	10—5-5	Griswold - - 8—6-11
Giles - - -	7—5-11	Grove - - - 4—11-2
Giovanni - -	10—7-3	Grover - - 4—11-11
Giralda - - -	7—11-5	Gus - - - - 11—3-8
Gladys - - -	5—8-6	Gussie - - - 8—8-9
Gloria - - -	8—7-1	Gustavus - - 22—7-6
Glen - - - -	2—5-6	Guthrie - - - 7—8-8
Glenn - - -	7—5-2	Guy - - - - 8—10-7
Glynn - - -	9—7-2	Gwendolyn - 11—9-11
Goldie - - -	7—2-5	Hale - - - 8—6-11
Gomez - - -	3—11-10	Halifax - - 7—11-5
Good - - -	5—3-11	Hall - - - - 6—1-5
Goodwin - -	6—3-3	Hallam - - - 2—2-9
Goodyear - -	9—9-9	Hamilton - - 11—7-22
Gordon - - -	10—3-7	Hamlin - - - 3—10-2
Gould - - -	5—9-5	Hammond - - 5—7-7
Grace - - -	7—6-10	Hamon - - - 6—7-8
Gracia - - -	3—11-10	Hancock - - - 10—7-3
Graham - - -	3—2-10	Hanes - - - 2—6-5
Granger - - -	7—6-10	Hanna - - - 2—2-9
Grant - - -	6—1-5	Hannah - - - 10—2-8
Granville - -	10—6-4	Hans - - - - 6—1-5

Hansen - - - 7—6-10	Helena - - - 9—11-7
Hanson - - - 8—7-10	Helmer - - - 7—10-6
Harding - - 7—10-6	Henri - - - 9—5-22
Hardy - - - 11—8-3	Henrici - - - 3—5-7
Hargrave - - 8—7-10	Henrietta - - 10—2-8
Harlan - - - 9—2-7	Henry - - - 7—3-22
Harlow - - - 5—7-7	Herbert - - - 4—10-3
Harold - - - 4—7-6	Herman - - - 5—6-8
Harper - - - 3—6-6	Hermes - - - 5—10-4
Harriet - - - 7—6-10	Herold - - - 8—11-6
Harris - - - 10—10-9	Herring - - 7—5-11
Harrison - - - 3—7-5	Hester - - - 3—10-2
Harry - - - 7—8-8	Hezekiah - - 10—2-8
Harvey - - - 7—6-10	Hicks - - - - 5—9-5
Harwood - - - 3—4-8	Hilda - - - - 7—1-6
Hattie - - - 9—6-3	Hilde - - - 11—5-6
Hauser - - - 9—9-9	Hill - - - - 5—9-5
Hawkins - - 4—10-3	Hiram - - - 4—10-3
Hawthorne - - 4—3-10	Hobart - - - 10—7-3
Hayden - - - 3—6-6	Hobson - - - 10—3-7
Haydn - - - 7—1-6	Hoffman - - 9—7-11
Hayes - - - 22—6-7	Homer - - - 5—11-3
Haynes - - - 9—6-3	Honore - - - 3—8-22
Hays - - - - 8—1-7	Honoria - - 8—22-22
Hayward - - - 8—2-6	Hope - - - 8—11-6
Hazel - - - 7—6-10	Horace - - - 5—3-2
Hazelton - - 11—3-8	Horatio - - 5—22-10
Heath - - - 6—6-9	Hortense - - - 5—7-7
Heber - - - 11—10-10	Hosea - - - - 3—3-9
Hector - - 6—11-22	Howard - - - 6—7-8
Hedwig - - - 11—5-6	Howell - - 3—11-10
Helen - - - 8—10-7	Hubbard - - 11—4-7

115

Hudson	- - -	9—9-9	Ivanhoe	- -	11—3-8
Hugh	- - - -	8—3-5	Jabez	- - -	8—6-11
Hugo	- - - -	6—9-6	Jack	- - - -	7—1-6
Hulda	- - -	10—4-6	Jackson	- - -	10—7-3
Hume	- - - -	2—8-3	Jacob	- - - -	4—7-6
Hunt	- - - -	9—3-6	Jacqueline	- -	7—5-2
Hunter	- - -	5—8-6	Jacques	- - -	22—9-4
Hyde	- - - -	6—3-3	James	- - -	3—6-6
Ibsen	- - -	22—5-8	Jane	- - - -	3—6-6
Ida	- - - -	5—10-4	Janet	- - - -	5—6-8
Ignatius	- -	10—22-6	Jarvis	- - -	7—10-6
Illinois	- - -	9—6-3	Jason	- - - -	5—7-7
Immanuel	- -	7—9-7	Jean	- - - -	3—6-6
Inez	- - - -	9—5-4	Jeanette	- - -	8—7-10
Ingersoll	- -	3—2-10	Jeanne	- -	22—11-11
Iole	- - - -	5—2-3	Jed	- - - -	10—5-5
Ione	- - - -	7—2-5	Jefferson	- -	8—7-10
Iowa	- - - -	3—7-5	Jeffries	- - -	6—10-5
Ira	- - - -	10—10-9	Jehu	- - - -	8—8-9
Irene	- - -	6—10-5	Jenkins	- - -	10—5-5
Irvin	- - - -	9—9-9	Jennie	- - -	3—10-11
Irving	- - -	7—9-7	Jenny	- - -	5—3-11
Isaac	- - -	6—11-4	Jeremiah	- -	6—2-22
Isabel	- - - -	3—6-6	Jeremy	- - -	4—8-5
Isabella	- - -	7—7-9	Jerome	- - -	3—7-5
Isabelle	- - -	11—2-9	Jerry	- - - -	4—3-1
Isadore	- - -	8—3-5	Jervis	- - -	11—5-6
Isaiah	- - -	11—2-9	Jesse	- - -	4—10-3
Ishmael	- -	4—6-7	Jessica	- - -	3—6-6
Isis	- - - -	2—9-2	Jessie	- - -	22—10-3
Israel	- - -	10—6-4	Jewel	- - -	10—10-9
Ivan	- - -	10—10-9	Joab	- - - -	10—7-3

Joachim - - - 5—7-7	Juno - - - - 6—9-6
Joan - - - - 4—7-6	Jupiter - - - 9—8-10
Joanna - - - 10—8-11	Justin - - - - 3—3-9
Joanne - - - 5—3-11	Kaiser - - - 9—6-3
Joash - - - 8—7-10	Karl - - - - 6—1-5
Job - - - - 9—6-3	Karol - - - - 3—7-5
Joe - - - - 3—11-1	Kate - - - - 10—6-4
Joel - - - - 6—11-4	Katha - - - - 5—2-3
John - - - - 2—6-5	Katherine - - 10—2-8
Johnson - - - 5—3-2	Kathryn - - - 7—8-8
Johnston - - 7—3-22	Katrina - - 11—11-9
Johnstone - - 3—8-22	Keith - - - - 8—5-3
Jonah - - - - 3—7-5	Kellogg - - 6—11-22
Jonas - - - - 5—7-7	Kelly - - - - 2—3-8
Jonathan - - 11—8-3	Ken - - - - 3—5-7
Jones - - - 9—11-7	Kennedy - - - 6—8-7
Jordan - - - 8—7-10	Kenneth - - 5—10-22
Josef - - - 10—11-8	Kent - - - - 5—5-9
Joseph - - - 10—11-8	Kenyon - - 3—11-10
Josephine - - 11—7-22	Kiev - - - - 2—5-6
Josephus - - - 5—5-9	King - - - - 5—9-5
Joshua - - - 2—10-10	Kingsley - - - 3—5-7
Josiah - - - 8—7-10	Kipling - - - 6—9-6
Judah - - - 8—4-4	Kirby - - - 11—7-4
Judas - - - 10—4-6	Kirk - - - 22—9-4
Judith - - - 9—3-6	Kirke - - - 9—5-4
Judson - - - 2—9-11	Kittie - - - 11—5-6
Juel - - - - 3—8-4	Kitty - - - 22—7-6
Julia - - - - 8—4-4	Knight - - - 6—9-6
Julian - - - 22—4-9	Knox - - - 10—6-4
Julien - - - - 8—8-9	Korah - - - 8—7-10
Julius - - - 2—6-5	Krishna - - - 8—10-7

Kruger - - - 8—8-9	Letha - - - 10—6-4
Kruse - - - - 2—8-3	Levi - - - - 3—5-7
Kyrle - - - 8—3-5	Lewis - - - - 5—5-9
Lafayette - - - 5—3-2	Lille - - - - 5—5-9
Laila - - - 8—11-6	Lillian - - - 6—10-5
Lalla - - - 11—2-9	Lillie - - - - 5—5-9
Landis - - - 5—10-4	Lily - - - - 22—7-6
Larry - - - 11—8-3	Lina - - - - 9—10-8
Launce - - - 2—9-11	Lincoln - - - 7—6-10
Laura - - - - 8—5-3	Lind - - - - 3—9-3
Laurens - - - 9—9-9	Linne - - - - 9—5-4
Lawrence - - - 9—11-7	Linnie - - - 9—5-4
Lea - - - - 9—6-3	Lionel - - - 4—2-11
Leah - - - - 8—6-11	Lloyd - - - 5—4-10
Lee - - - - 4—10-3	Locke - - 10—11-8
Leigh - - - 5—5-9	Lodge - - - 7—11-5
Leighton - - - 9—2-7	Logan - - - 22—7-6
Leland - - - 3—6-6	Lois - - - - 10—6-4
Lemuel - - - 5—4-10	London - - - 11—3-8
Lena - - - - 5—6-8	Long - - - - 3—6-6
Lenna - - - 10—6-4	Loomis - - - 11—3-8
Lenora - - - 11—3-8	Lopez - - - 11—11-9
Leo - - - - 5—11-3	Loren - - - 10—11-8
Leon - - - 10—11-8	Loretta - - - 10—3-7
Leonard - - - 6—3-3	Lottie - - - - 9—2-7
Leonardo - - - 3—9-3	Lou - - - - 3—3-9
Leonidas - - - 7—3-4	Louis - - - 22—9-4
Leonore - - - 3—22-8	Louisa - - - 5—10-4
Leopold - - - 7—8-8	Louise - - - 9—5-4
Leroy - - - - 3—9-3	Lowell - - - 7—11-5
Leslie - - - 8—10-7	Lucia - - - 10—4-6
Lester - - - 7—10-6	Lucian - - - 6—4-11

Lucifer - - - 11—8-3	Margaret - - 11—7-4
Lucius - - - 22—6-7	Marguerite - - 9—5-4
Lucretia - - - 8—9-8	Maria - - - 6—11-4
Lucy - - - 7—10-6	Marian - - - 11—11-9
Ludwig - - - 4—3-10	Marianne - - - 3—7-5
Luke - - - - 4—8-5	Marie - - - 10—6-4
Lura - - - - 7—4-3	Marietta - - - 6—7-8
Luria - - - - 7—4-3	Marion - - - 7—7-9
Lydia - - - - 6—8-7	Marius - - - 9—4-5
Lynch - - - 8—7-10	Marjorie - - - 8—3-5
Lyons - - - 22—4-9	Mark - - - - 7—1-6
Lytton - - - 7—4-3	Marlow - - - 10—7-3
Macleod - - - 8—3-5	Marquette - - 3—5-7
Madden - - - 5—6-8	Marquis - - - 8—4-22
Madeline - - - 9—2-7	Marshall - - 3—2-10
Madelon - - 10—3-7	Martha - - - 7—2-5
Madison - - - 3—7-5	Martin - - - 3—10-2
Mae - - - 10—6-4	Martina - - - 4—11-2
Maggie - - - 6—6-9	Martinez - - 7—6-10
Magnus - - - 3—4-8	Martini - - - 3—10-2
Maison - - - 8—7-10	Martyn - - - 10—8-2
Major - - - 3—7-5	Marx - - - 2—1-10
Malcolm - - - 6—7-8	Mary - - - - 3—8-4
Mame - - - 5—6-8	Masie - - - - 2—6-5
Manlius - - - 8—4-4	Mason - - - 8—7-10
Manning - - 9—10-8	Mat - - - - 7—1-6
Mansfield - - 11—6-5	Mathew - - 7—6-10
Manuel - - - 3—9-3	Mathews - - - 8—6-2
Marcella - - 11—7-22	Mathias - - - 8—11-6
Marcellus - - 5—9-5	Matilda - - - 6—11-4
Marcia - - - 9—11-7	Matthew - - - 9—6-3
Marcus - - - 3—4-8	Mattie - - - - 5—6-8

Maud - - - - 3—4-8	Mills - - - 2—9-11
Maude - - - 8—9-8	Milton - - - 11—6-5
Maurice - - - 7—9-7	Mina - - - 10—10-9
Max - - - 11—1-10	Minerva - - 10—6-22
Maximilian - 6—11-22	Minnie - - - 10—5-5
Maxine - - - 3—6-6	Mira - - - 5—10-4
Maxwell - - - 9—6-3	Mirabel - - - 6—6-9
May - - - - 3—1-11	Miranda - - 6—11-22
Mayme - - - 3—6-6	Miriam - - - 9—10-8
Mayo - - - 9—7-11	Mirza - - - 4—10-3
Mazeppa - - - 6—7-8	Mitzi - - - - 5—9-5
Mead - - - - 5—6-8	Moab - - - - 4—7-6
Meade - - - 10—11-8	Modjeska - - - 6—3-3
Media - - - - 5—6-8	Mohammed - - 9—3-6
Melba - - - - 6—6-9	Moliere - - - 5—7-7
Melissa - - - 6—6-9	Mollie - - - 3—2-10
Melita - - - 6—6-9	Molly - - - 5—4-10
Melville - - 9—10-8	Mona - - - - 7—7-9
Melvin - - - 3—5-7	Monica - - 10—7-3
Mercedes - - - 9—6-3	Montague - - 6—6-9
Mercer - - - 8—10-7	Monte - - 22—11-11
Meredith - - 10—10-9	Montgomery - 10—6-4
Merle - - - 8—10-7	Monticello - - 10—8-2
Merlin - - - 8—5-3	Moody - - - 9—10-8
Merton - - - 4—11-2	Moore - - - 3—8-4
Merwin - - 10—5-5	Moran - - - 7—7-9
Michael - - - 6—6-9	Mordecai - - - 5—3-2
Michel - - - 5—5-9	Morgan - - - 5—7-7
Mike - - - - 2—5-6	Morrill - - - 7—6-10
Miller - - - 6—5-10	Morris - - - 11—6-5
Millicent - - - 7—5-2	Morrison - - 4—3-10
Millie - - - 6—5-10	Morse - - - 7—11-5

Morton	- - -	5—3-2	Nemesis	- -	3—10-11
Moses	- - -	8—11-6	Neptune	- -	5—4-10
Mother	- - -	7—11-5	Nero	- - -	7—11-5
Mozart	- - -	3—7-5	Nettie	- - -	10—10-9
Muratore	- - -	3—6-6	Neva	- - - -	6—6-9
Murdock	- -	4—9-22	Neville	- - -	7—10-6
Muriel	- - -	6—8-7	Newton	- -	10—11-8
Murphy	- -	11—10-10	Nicholas	- - -	9—7-2
Myra	- - - -	3—8-4	Nichols	- - -	8—6-2
Myron	- - -	4—4-9	Nicholson	- -	10—3-7
Nada	- - -	11—2-9	Nick	- - -	10—9-10
Nadine	- - -	11—6-5	Nicol	- - -	8—6-11
Nahum	- - -	3—4-8	Nina	- - -	2—10-10
Nala	- - -	10—2-8	Nirvana	- - -	7—11-5
Nan	- - -	11—1-10	Noah	- - - -	2—7-4
Nancy	- - -	3—8-4	Noel	- - -	10—11-8
Nannie	- - -	3—6-6	Nola	- - - -	6—7-8
Naomi	- - -	7—7-9	Nona	- - -	8—7-10
Napoleon	- -	11—9-2	Nordica	- - -	10—7-3
Narcissa	- -	3—11-10	Norma	- - -	7—7-9
Natalie	- - -	8—7-10	Norman	- - -	3—7-5
Nathalie	- - -	7—7-9	Norris	- - -	3—6-6
Nathan	- - -	22—2-2	Norton	- - -	6—3-3
Nathaniel	- - -	3—7-5	Novello	- - -	5—8-6
Neal	- - - -	5—6-8	Nye	- - - -	8—3-5
Ned	- - - -	5—5-9	Nysa	- - - -	5—8-6
Neil	- - - -	22—5-8	Obadiah	- - -	4—8-5
Neiva	- - - -	6—6-9	Oberon	- - -	6—8-7
Nell	- - - -	7—5-11	O'Brien	- - -	9—2-7
Nella	- - -	8—6-11	O'Bryan	- - -	3—5-7
Nellie	- - -	3—10-11	O'Connell	- -	9—8-10
Nelson	- - -	7—11-5	O'Connor	- -	4—9-22

Octave	- - -	3—3-9
Octavia	- - -	8—8-9
Octavius	- -	11—10-10
Odessa	- - -	9—3-6
O'Donnell	- -	10—8-2
Oglesby	- - -	4—9-4
Olaf	- - - -	7—7-9
Ole	- - - -	5—11-3
Olga	- - -	8—7-10
Olin	- - - -	5—6-8
Oliva	- - - -	5—7-7
Olive	- - - -	9—2-7
Oliver	- - -	9—2-7
Olivia	- - -	5—7-7
Oman	- - -	7—7-9
Omar	- - - -	2—7-4
Omer	- - -	6—11-4
Ona	- - - -	3—7-5
O'Neil	- - -	10—2-8
Ora	- - - -	7—7-9
Orel	- - -	5—11-3
Orlando	- - -	7—4-3
Orleans	- - -	3—3-9
Orloff	- - -	9—3-6
Orpheus	- - -	3—5-7
Orville	- - -	3—2-10
Oscar	- - - -	2—7-4
Osgood	- - -	3—9-3
Oswald	- - -	2—7-4
Otho	- - -	22—3-10
Otis	- - - -	9—6-3
Otto	- - - -	7—3-4

Owen	- - -	3—11-10
Page	- - - -	2—6-5
Paine	- - - -	9—6-3
Palmer	- - -	11—6-5
Pamela	- - -	3—7-5
Panches	- - -	3—6-6
Pancho	- - -	3—7-5
Pandora	- - -	6—8-7
Park	- - -	10—1-9
Parker	- - -	6—6-9
Parry	- - - -	6—8-7
Pascal	- - - -	7—2-5
Paterson	- - -	9—3-6
Patterson	- -	11—3-8
Patti	- - -	3—10-11
Patton	- - -	5—7-7
Paul	- - - -	5—4-10
Paula	- - -	6—5-10
Paulina	- - -	11—5-6
Pauline	- - -	6—9-6
Pavia	- - -	22—11-11
Payne	- - -	7—6-10
Pearl	- - -	7—6-10
Pedro	- - -	4—11-2
Pembroke	- - -	4—7-6
Penn	- - - -	22—5-8
Pepys	- - - -	9—3-6
Percival	- - -	5—6-8
Percy	- - -	4—3-10
Perkins	- - -	11—5-6
Perry	- - -	10—3-7
Peter	- - -	10—10-9

Peters - - 11—10-10	Primrose - - - 5—2-3
Petersen - - - 3—6-6	Prince - - - 11—5-6
Peterson - - - 4—7-6	Princess - - - 4—5-8
Petra - - - - 6—6-9	Priscilla - - 9—10-8
Pharoah - - - 4—8-5	Procter - - - 5—11-3
Phelps - - - 4—5-8	Proctor - - - 6—3-3
Phenix - - - 4—5-8	Prudence - - 5—4-10
Philemon - - 11—2-9	Psyche - - - 4—3-10
Philip - - - - 7—9-7	Queen - - - 8—4-4
Phillip - - - 10—9-10	Queenie - - - 4—9-4
Phillippa - - 9—10-8	Quentin - - 10—8-2
Phillips - - 11—9-11	Quincy - - - 8—10-7
Philo - - - - 6—6-9	Quirk - - - 4—3-10
Phipps - - - 3—9-3	Rachel - - - 11—6-5
Phyllis - - - 11—7-22	Radcliffe - - 10—6-4
Pierce - - 11—10-10	Rae - - - - 6—6-9
Pierre - - - 8—10-7	Raleigh - - - 6—6-9
Pierrot - - - 11—2-9	Ralph - - - 10—1-9
Pike - - - - 5—5-9	Ramah - - - 5—2-3
Pinto - - - 11—6-5	Ramona - - - 8—8-9
Pizarro - - - 4—7-6	Randall - - - 8—2-6
Plato - - - 10—7-3	Randolph - - - 7—7-9
Pliny - - - - 4—7-6	Raphael - - - 7—7-9
Pluto - - - - 3—9-3	Rawlins - - 6—10-5
Pocahontas - - 4—5-8	Rawson - - - 9—7-2
Poe - - - - 9—11-7	Ray - - - - 8—1-7
Pola - - - - 8—7-10	Raymond - - 9—7-11
Polla - - - - 2—7-4	Read - - - 10—6-4
Polly - - - - 8—4-4	Reade - - - 6—11-4
Porter - - - 11—11-9	Rebecca - - 10—11-8
Potter - - - 4—11-2	Red - - - - 9—5-4
Powell - - - 11—11-9	Reed - - - 5—10-4

Reeves - - - 11—6-5	Rolfe - - - 11—11-9
Regan - - - 9—6-3	Rolla - - - 22—7-6
Reggie - - - 6—10-5	Rolle - - - 8—11-6
Reggio - - - 7—2-5	Rollo - - - - 9—3-6
Regina - - - 9—6-3	Roman - - - 7—7-9
Reid - - - - 9—5-4	Romeo - - - 3—8-4
Reinhart - - - 3—6-6	Romulus - - 11—3-8
Rembrandt - - 5—6-8	Roosevelt - - 5—22-10
Remus - - - 22—8-5	Rosa - - - 8—7-10
Rene - - - 6—10-5	Rosalie - - - 7—3-4
Reno - - - 7—11-5	Rosalind - - 11—7-22
Reuben - - - 11—4-7	Rosaline - - - 3—3-9
Reva - - - 10—6-4	Rosamond - - 9—4-5
Reynolds - - 4—11-11	Roscoe - - - 3—8-4
Rhea - - - - 5—6-8	Rose - - - 3—11-10
Rhodes - - - 6—11-22	Rosetta - - - 8—3-5
Richard - - - 7—10-6	Rosini - - - 3—6-6
Richelieu - - - 9—4-5	Ross - - - - 8—6-11
Ring - - - - 3—9-3	Roth - - - 7—6-10
Robert - - 6—11-22	Roxana - - - 10—8-2
Roberta - - - 7—3-22	Roy - - - - 22—4-9
Roberts - - - 7—11-5	Ruben - - - 6—8-7
Robins - - - 5—6-8	Rudolf - - - 4—9-22
Robinson - - 7—3-22	Rudolph - - - 4—9-4
Robson - - - 11—3-8	Rupert - - - 8—8-9
Roderick - - 11—2-9	Ruskin - - - 11—3-8
Roderigo - - 10—8-11	Russell - - - 7—8-8
Rodgers - - - 5—11-3	Ruth - - - 22—3-10
Rodin - - - - 6—6-9	Rutherford - - 7—5-11
Rodriguez - - 6—5-10	Ryan - - - 22—8-5
Roger - - - 9—11-7	Sade - - - - 11—6-5
Roland - - - 10—7-3	Sadie - - - - 2—6-5

Sadler - - - - 5—6-8	Shelby - - - 8—3-5
Salina - - - 2—11-9	Sheldon - - - 5—11-3
Salome - - - 2—3-8	Sheridan - - - 6—6-9
Sam - - - - 6—1-5	Sherman - - - 6—6-9
Sambo - - - 5—7-7	Silvester - - - 3—10-2
Samson - - - 9—7-11	Silvia - - - 9—10-8
Samuel - - - 8—9-8	Simon - - - 7—6-10
Sancho - - - 6—7-8	Simpson - - - 6—6-9
Sandford - - 9—7-11	Sloan - - - - 7—7-9
Sando - - - 8—7-10	Sloane - - - 3—3-9
Sandy - - - 9—8-10	Smith - - - - 6—9-6
Sanford - - - 5—7-7	Smyth - - - 22—7-6
Sappho - - - 3—7-5	Sofia - - - - 5—7-7
Sara - - - - 3—2-10	Solomon - - - 4—9-4
Sarah - - - - 2—2-9	Sophia - - - - 5—7-7
Sargent - - - 3—6-6	Sophie - - - 9—2-7
Sari - - - 2—10-10	Sophronia - - 7—22-3
Saul - - - - 8—4-4	Sousa - - - 3—10-2
Saunders - - 11—9-2	Spence - - - 8—10-7
Scot - - - - 3—6-6	Sprague - - - 6—9-6
Scott - - - - 5—6-8	Stanley - - - 6—6-9
Sebastian - - 9—7-11	Stella - - - - 6—6-9
Selina - - - - 6—6-9	Stephen - - - 6—10-5
Selma - - - - 5—6-8	Stephens - - 7—10-6
Selwyn - - - 8—3-5	Steve - - - 8—10-7
Sergius - - - 8—8-9	Steven - - - 22—10-3
Seth - - - - 7—5-11	Stevens - - - 5—10-4
Seton - - - 10—11-8	Sterling - - - 5—5-9
Seward - - - 7—6-10	Stewart - - - 7—6-10
Shakespeare - - 9—8-10	Stokes - - - 8—11-6
Sharp - - - - 8—1-7	Stone - - - 10—11-8
Sheba - - - 8—6-11	Stuart - - - - 9—4-5

Sue - - - -	9—8-1	Timothy - -	11—22-7
Sullivan - - -	11—4-7	Tindal - - -	6—10-5
Sumner - - -	9—8-10	Todd - - -	7—6-10
Susan - - -	11—4-7	Tolstoi - - -	11—3-8
Susie - - -	10—8-2	Tom - - - -	3—6-6
Suzanne - -	10—9-10	Tommy - -	5—4-10
Sylvester - -	10—8-2	Tompkins - -	9—6-3
Sylvia - - - -	7—8-8	Topsy - - -	5—4-10
Tabitha - - -	7—11-5	Tracy - - -	22—8-5
Tacie - - - -	2—6-5	Trent - - - -	5—5-9
Tad - - - -	7—1-6	Trilby - - -	5—7-7
Taft - - -	11—1-10	Tucker - - -	6—8-7
Talmage - - -	5—7-7	Tyler - - - -	8—3-5
Ted - - - -	11—5-6	Tyndall - - -	7—8-8
Terry - - - -	5—3-2	Tyrol - - -	9—4-5
Texas - - -	6—6-9	Ulrich - - -	8—3-5
Thaddeus - -	10—9-10	Underwood - -	11—2-9
Thais - - -	3—10-11	Upton - - -	5—9-5
Thalia - - -	6—11-4	Uranus - - -	22—7-6
Thanet - - -	5—6-8	Uriel - - -	11—8-3
Thelma - - -	5—6-8	Ursula - - -	2—7-4
Theodora - - -	5—9-5	Valentine - -	3—2-10
Theodore - -	9—22-5	Valeria - - -	5—7-7
Theresa - - -	4—11-2	Valla - - -	3—2-10
Theron - - -	8—11-6	Vanderbilt - -	8—6-11
Thirza - -	10—10-9	Vandyke - - -	10—4-6
Thomas - - -	22—7-6	Venus - - -	9—8-10
Thora - - -	8—7-10	Vera - - -	10—6-4
Thoreau - -	7—6-10	Verden - -	5—10-22
Thurston - - -	9—9-9	Verdie - - -	9—10-8
Tibbie - - -	11—5-6	Vergil - - -	10—5-5
Tillie - - - -	4—5-8	Vern - - - -	5—5-9

126

Verna - - -	6—6-9	
Verne - - -	10—10-9	
Vernon - - -	7—11-5	
Verona - - -	3—3-9	
Veronica - - -	6—3-3	
Vesta - - - -	4—6-7	
Victor - - -	6—6-9	
Victoria - - -	7—7-9	
Violet - - -	11—2-9	
Virgil - - - -	5—9-5	
Virginia - -	8—10-7	
Vishnu - - -	3—3-9	
Vivian - - -	5—10-4	
Volga - - - -	3—7-5	
Voltaire - - -	3—3-9	
Vonda - - - -	2—7-4	
Vondel - - -	9—11-7	
Wade - - - -	6—6-9	
Wagner - - -	5—6-8	
Waldemar - -	5—7-7	
Walden - - -	5—6-8	
Waldo - - -	10—7-3	
Walker - - -	7—6-10	
Wallace - - -	3—7-5	
Waller - - -	8—6-2	
Walsh - - -	9—1-8	
Walter - - -	7—6-10	
Wanamaker - -	6—8-7	
Ward - - -	10—1-9	
Warfield - - -	6—6-9	
Warner - - -	7—6-10	
Warren - - -	7—6-10	

Washington - -	4—7-6	
Watts - - -	11—1-10	
Waverly - - -	7—4-3	
Wayland - - -	8—2-6	
Webster - -	11—10-10	
Wellington - -	5—2-3	
Wells - - - -	8—5-3	
Wesley - - -	8—10-7	
West - - - -	4—5-8	
Whalen - - -	9—6-3	
Wheeler - - -	4—6-7	
White - - -	11—5-6	
Whitman - -	7—10-6	
Whyte - - -	9—3-6	
Wilber - - -	6—5-10	
Wilbur - - -	4—3-10	
Wilhelm - -	10—5-5	
Wilhelmina -	7—6-10	
Wilkes - - -	7—5-11	
Wilkins - - -	7—9-7	
William - -	7—10-6	
Williams - -	8—10-7	
Willis - - - -	3—9-3	
Wilma - -	22—10-3	
Wilson - - -	11—6-5	
Winifred - -	7—5-11	
Winnie - - -	11—5-6	
Winslow - -	7—6-10	
Winston - - -	6—6-9	
Winthrop - -	6—6-9	
Wright - - -	4—9-4	
Xanthippe - -	5—6-8	

Xaver - - - 7—6-10	Zachariah - - 3—3-9
Xavier - - - 7—6-10	Zacharias - - 5—3-11
Xenia - - - 8—6-11	Zadok - - - 3—7-5
Xenophon - - 3—8-4	Zella - - - - 2—6-5
Xerxes - - - 5—10-22	Zeno - - - - 6—11-4
Yates - - - 7—6-10	Zenobia - - - 9—3-6
York - - - - 6—6-9	Zephon - - 3—11-10
Young - - - 10—9-10	Zephyr - - - 8—3-5
Yvette - - - 7—8-8	Zerlina - - - 4—6-7
Yvon - - - 22—4-9	Zeus - - - - 8—8-9
Yvonne - - - 5—9-5	Zollner - - 3—11-10
Zaccheus - - - 5—9-5	Zora - - - - 6—7-8

128

Made in United States
North Haven, CT
22 November 2023